BREAKING THE CHAINS OF

UNFORGIVENESS

8 STEPS ON HOW TO LET GO OF BITTERNESS AND STEP INTO YOUR GREATNESS

PHIL SIBANDA

One minute of anger can weaken your immune system for hours and one minute of laughter can boost your immune system for a day. Laughter is the best medicine of all time.

It is the time to ACT:

Accept the Past
Change the Present
Transform the Future

Contents

Introduction

Life is full of challenges that can potentially make us angry and bitter and, as a result, we end up finding it difficult to forgive. Some of the things that happen in our lives are not fair and they will always remain unfair. When we allow things like anger and bitterness to take root on the inside of us, this usually results in struggling with forgiveness. Bitterness is always the root cause of unwillingness to forgive. Things like anger, wrath, clamour and malice are all the offspring or brothers and cousins of bitterness. We were born to be loving people; we were born to love and to be loved, but bitterness and unforgiveness have robbed most people in the world of living and experiencing a joyful life. Do not be a slave of unforgiveness; forgive to be free and enjoy life.

The major question is: How do I forgive people who have hurt me so much in life? What must I do to be able to forgive and live a normal happy life? This book will present you with a number of different ways that can help you to learn how to forgive and live a happy life. Millions and millions of people today are struggling with the spirit of unforgiveness and, as a result, they become a slave to those people who are holding grudges against them. It is believed that many diseases in the world today are directly linked to, or as a result of unforgiveness. It is time for you to forgive and live a healthier life; you deserve a better life than being a slave of other people's injustices in your life. God wants to set you free as you are reading this book. This is your set time to let go of the past and let God open a new page in your life.

This book, Breaking the Chains of Unforgiveness, will help you to be able to break the chains of unforgiveness and to eliminate all root causes of unforgiveness. I will take you through an insight into the causes of unforgiveness step by step by looking deeper into bitterness, which is the root cause of all problems related to unforgiveness. In this book, I will reveal to you the ways that will help you to be set free from every chain of unforgiveness. The ways of setting yourself free from the chain of unforgiveness are not difficult and complicated; most of them are principles set in the word of God and some of them are the ones that I have experienced in my life from childhood to present time working as a pastor.

So many people are taking medication, some are in sick beds and some have sadly died because they are not willing to forgive. It has been discovered that some of the diseases related to heart conditions, chronicle back pain, serious mental health conditions, and the emotional physical consequences are because of unforgiveness. Unforgiveness and bitterness turn your immune system inside out and make you vulnerable to diseases. Our God is a loving God. He wants to see us living a happy, joyful and loving life. The definition of our God is love, so if we are saving Him, He expects us to abide by his principles. As you read this book, believe that your time has come to be set free from any chains of unforgiveness in Jesus' name. It does not matter how long the chains of unforgiveness have bound you, because everything that has a beginning does has an end. As you read this book, I believe that your time to be set free has come. Just believe and follow every step to your freedom and you shall be set free. We have been created in the image of God and our lives must reflect the nature of our Father, which is the nature of love.

How do I break the chains of unforgiveness? First, you need to understand the stages of bitterness and how to uproot the root causes of bitterness. Secondly, you must understand what God says about forgiveness. You can live a life that is free from being bound with the chains of unforgiveness by understanding the following:

1. Understanding the causes of bitterness
2. Understanding the stages of bitterness
3. How do I come out of the cycle of bitterness?

4. How do I let go of the past?
5. What does the Bible say about forgiveness?
6. Living the life that God has intended for you

Most of the people in the world today are battling with the problem of unforgiveness. They find it difficult to forgive people who hurt them in life and, as a result, they find themselves bound by the chains of unforgiveness. Some people are trying to fight the fruits of unforgiveness instead of destroying the root causes of bitterness. In this book, I will explain each principle in depth, how they can help you to deal with the spirit of unforgiveness and you are going to understand why most people are struggling to overcome bitterness.

It is time to get prepared! You are about to begin a process that will help you to uproot all the root causes of bitterness and unforgiveness and you are going to be able to identify where you are in terms of the stages of bitterness. I can assure you that following these principles of dealing with bitterness and unforgiveness will help you to live a life free from strife, which is a life of peace, joy, love and a life of fulfilment according to God's plan and resemblance.

Breaking the chains of unforgiveness is all about dealing with the root causes of unforgiveness by identifying the source of bitterness and how to deal with its causes step by step. Gradually, this will lead you to total freedom from the oppression of the spirit of unforgiveness. As you read this book, I trust God that He will open your understanding about how to deal with the issues that have caused you to be bitter, and He is faithful to set you free from every bondage of bitterness.

Part 1.
What Is Bitterness and What Are the Causes of It?

Chapter 1.

Bitterness and Its Causes

31. 'Get rid of all bitterness and wrath and anger and clamour and slander be put away from you, along with all malice (all types of evil behaviour).'

– Ephesians 4:31(KJV).

From this scripture above, we see that bitterness is the word that is mentioned first before the rest of the list of behaviours. As indicated from the scripture, bitterness is the spring or the root cause of all sort of problems related to unforgiveness. Bitterness is actually the negative attitude that makes people refuse to forgive others or to be forgiven, and as a result, it shuts all doors to reconciliation with other people. A sign of someone with bitterness is expressed in the form of harshness, spitefulness, shouting and resentment. Like a tree or any plant, it does have roots, a stem and branches, and the branches carry the fruits. The tree cannot survive without the roots; the life of the tree depends on its roots that supply the necessary nutrients for the tree to grow and produce the right fruits.

The tree cannot grow without the roots, and it is the same way with our lives. If we do not get rid of bitterness, which is the root cause of anger, wrath, clamour and malice, we will have a problem with unforgiveness. This will lead us to live a miserable life, which is against the will of God. Remember that a bitter root will always produce a bitter fruit, so if you hold or harbour bitterness within yourself it will be seen through your actions or behaviour. As you know that a root develops from a seed, so what makes one bitter is a seed which is originally an offence. The offence can be anything ranging from someone saying words to you that you do not like, it can be a negative comment, or it can be at work, when you have trained a particular person but to your amazement, that person gets promoted to be your senior. How are you going to feel? Here are some things that can cause people to be bitter:

1. When someone that you trusted so much has betrayed you.
2. When you have been abused by people who were supposed to protect you.
3. When people are judging you wrongly.
4. When you have experienced a broken relationship or divorce.
5. Maybe you have been sexually, verbally and physically abused as an innocent child. The list goes on and on.

All these things can be a seed of offence and, if you do not let it go, the root of bitterness will take its place in your life. Challenge yourself by getting rid of all bitterness, as the above scripture says, so that you can enjoy the life God intended for you. The big question is how do I let go of the painful things that people have done to me? Firstly, you need to be able to identify those things that have caused you to be bitter, because without identifying the root causes of your bitterness, it will be totally impossible to uproot them from your life. Just like a tree, you can take as many fruits or all the fruits from a tree as you can, but as long as the tree is still rooted, it is going to produce some more fruits in a matter of time. It is very important in your life to understand what caused you to be bitter, as that will help you to deal with the roots of your situation rather than the fruits of it. When you cut the roots of a tree, the tree will die. The same principle works in dealing with bitterness that results in unforgiveness. Dealing with bitterness is mostly a process because the strength of bitterness depends on how long you have been nurturing that bitterness. Usually, bitterness is nurtured when you do not want to let go of what has happened to you, and by taking secret delight in plotting revenge. You can get a breakthrough by breaking a cycle of negative thoughts of taking delight in planning revenge and by forgiving those people who have hurt you. When you forgive them, you are setting yourself free.

> *14. 'For if you forgive men their trespasses, your heavenly Father will also forgive you.*
>
> *15. But if you do not forgive men their trespasses, neither will your Father forgive your trespasses.'*

– Matthew 6: 14, 15 (KJV).

As the above scripture says, we need to forgive all the people who offend us in order for us to be forgiven by the Father in heaven. Sometimes we pray, and our prayers are not answered because we are holding onto bitterness. As I said before that bitterness is an attitude of not being willing to forgive or to be forgiven. The word of God tells us that we need to forgive others for God to forgive us. Most of the prayers we pray to God are not answered because of unforgiveness we have against the people who have done us wrong. Now is the time to forgive all the people who have hurt you, and set yourself free and that will open doors for your prayers to be answered.

When you do not forgive or let go of what has offended you, it develops to the next stage, which is anger. Anger is a signal that something is not right and it needs to be addressed. Always remember that anger is a normal and a good emotion when addressed quickly. When you are angry, it is the time when you show or express your displeasure about something that affects you, and the purpose of this anger is to motivate you to deal with your challenge quickly.

26. 'And "don't sin by letting anger control you." Do not let the sun go down while you are still angry,

27. For anger gives a mighty foothold to the devil' (NLT).

– Ephesians 4:26, 27 (NLT).

When we carefully examine the scripture above, you will notice that the Bible does not say do not sin by getting angry, but it says do not sin by allowing anger to control you. From this scripture, we learn that anger is a right emotion, which is there to help us to deal with something quickly. Anger becomes a wrong emotion if you keep it too long inside of you, which is why the Bible warns us not to let the sun go down while you are still angry. When you do not deal quickly with the issues that have made you angry, then that anger becomes a weapon of plotting secret revenge. When you do not forgive quickly, then that anger becomes a loophole that the devil will use to destroy your life and those around you. When you do not deal with anger quickly then it develops to other more dangerous stages. When

17

you do not deal with what has made you angry the same day or as soon as possible as the Bible says, then that anger will start to control you. The anger that is not dealt with will develop into wrath, which is expressing your anger in the form of erupting like a volcano. This stage is when you start to scream and shout at people in a violent manner, which is out of your control. When your anger has reached this stage, you must realise that you are bottling up issues that have not been dealt with at an early stage, and now they are beginning to control you. This is a crucial stage where you are supposed to take drastic measures to eradicate any bitterness and resentment that you have allowed to stay inside of you.

When wrath is not dealt with, then it develops into clamour, which is a stage that makes one speak raging or evil words with intent to hurt others. This is the stage where you start quarrelling using venomous and harsh words directed to cause more harm to your so-called opponent. When you have reached this stage of clamour, you do not have any place of kindness in your life anymore, and you do not mind anymore what your words will do to the person you are expressing your anger to. When things are not dealt with at this stage of clamour, then it develops to a final and more dangerous stage called malice. This stage of malice is when you have reached a stage where you are prepared to injure someone as a solution to deal with your situation. This is where a final evil act is carried out; for example, you hear that a man has killed his wife or vice versa; this is an act caused by malice. All of the root causes of these stages I have been talking about are as a result of bitterness, which is the unwillingness to forgive and to be forgiven. Refuse today to be controlled by bitterness, anger, wrath, clamour and malice. Pray the following prayer with me for a change in your life:

Prayer:

Father, in the name of Jesus I command anything that you

Did not plant in my life to be uprooted right now. You spirit

Of bitterness, anger, wrath, clamour and malice, you are a

Name, which is not from my Father in heaven, therefore, I

Command you to bow under the mightily matchless name of

Jesus. I declare and decree that you have no more power and

Authority over my life any more, and I am free from your bondage.

In Jesus', name AMEN

13. 'Be even-tempered, content with second place, quick to forgive an offence. Forgive as quickly and completely as the Master forgave you.'

– Colossians 3:13 (NIV).

The above scripture is also talking about forgiving an offence quickly because that is the only way that we can live the free, happy and joyful life that God has planned for us. When you are holding onto bitterness, anger; wrath, clamour and malice, you will realise that you are a slave to those people who have offended you. Why can you not forgive today and set yourself free from the chains of unforgiveness? We are living in a world, and in times where life is not going to be fair to us every time. As long as you are living in this world, people will hurt you, treat you unfairly, falsely accuse you, cheat, belittle you and do other painful things to you, but always remember to forgive quickly. Do not allow bitterness to take root inside of you; forgive and set yourself free. When you are struggling with forgiveness, remind yourself that you have fallen short of Gods' glory but He has forgiven you several times and He still loves you despite what you have done. Always remember that the longer you take to let go, the harder it will be for you to forgive, which means the longer you hold resentment, the deeper that root of bitterness grows inside of you. When you forgive anyone who has offended you or hurt you, you are actually releasing all the pain, hurt and bitterness they have caused in your life. When you are holding onto bitterness most of the time, life becomes hard, meaningless and a struggle, because you are carrying all the junk and the weight of bitterness.

Forgiveness is always a choice, not an option. When I am giving counselling, I have had many people saying words like, 'I am not going to forgive them until they apologise to me'. They forget that forgiveness has to do more with them and their lives. When you do not forgive, the person who is going to be hurt the most is you. Whether the people who hurt you apologise or not, you are supposed to forgive them to set yourself free. Have you ever realised that most of the people who you are holding bitterness against are living their lives as normal and they are not even bothered about how you feel about them? Some of them do not even know that they have offended you. They have hurt you so much but the key to living a life that God intended for you, the life of joy, peace, love and freedom, is all based on forgiving them. Whenever you are holding bitterness against the people who hurt you, you are allowing them to live in your mind rent-free. You may say 'they hurt me so much I cannot forgive them under any circumstances', but one thing that you do not realise is that you are allowing them to hurt you day after day, week after week, month after month in your mind. Whenever you think about how people have hurt you, your mind immediately sends signals to the rest of your body and, as a result, the wounds will remain fresh and bleeding with the pain as if it happened at that moment. As long as you do not forgive, you will live in the perpetual pain of the past and in the shadow of the life you are supposed to live.

There was a study that was carried out which revealed that 70% of the people we meet in the street are holding onto bitterness, Just imagine that such a high percentage of people are robbing themselves from living a life that God has intended for them, the life of joy, peace, love and freedom. It is so amazing that 70% of the people you meet in the street are actual slaves to the people who hurt them or caused them pain. Why do you not start to forgive today and set yourself free from being a slave of the people who hurt you? They are enjoying their lives to the fullest while you are a slave or bound to their actions against you by an emotional link that is stronger than an iron bar. There is something that I realised about unforgiveness; people who do not want to forgive by holding onto bitterness are in a self-made prison where they are both the inmate and the jailer or prison warder at the same time. What I mean by this is that forgiveness is a choice; the moment you choose not to forgive, you have put yourself in your own self-made prison where you have the choice of either setting yourself free or staying in as a prisoner. Whenever you forgive, you are setting a prisoner free and you will realise that the prisoner is you.

Unforgiveness is like a big wall that is standing between where you are and where God wants you to be, which is a place of joy, peace, love and total freedom. When you forgive, that wall is removed and you will be able to become who God says you are. Our God is a loving and forgiving God, so He requires us to have his nature. We make mistakes repeatedly, yet He forgives our shortcomings and He still loves us. The things that we encounter in life can make us better or they can make us bitter. I encourage you today not to be bitter about your past hurts and pains, but to learn from your past emotional wounds and become a better person. Remember that life experiences will always be the best teachers in our lives.

All Things Work Together for Good

28. 'And we know that all things work
together for good to them that love God, to
them that are called according to His
purpose.'

– Romans 8:28 (KJV).

The scripture above is encouraging us that all things work together for good. It does not say some but it says all, which includes all the good things and all the pains and hurt that people have caused you; God is able to turn them to good use. You may have been abused verbally, physically and emotionally, but if you learn to forgive, God is able to use you to change other people who are going through what you have experienced in your life. Some of the things we go through in life are just a ministry in the making; all of them are there to equip us for where God is taking us. It may have been painful, embarrassing and shameful, but remember that as a chosen child of God, He is able to use your past pain and hurt to be a healing and a blessing to other people as long as you can forgive and let go of bitterness. When you get a revelation of the above scripture, you will realise that there is no need to be bitter about how people have hurt you or caused pain in your life, but you will understand that God can change your negative experiences to be something good in your life. Some of the negative experiences we encounter in life God has allowed to happen so that He can teach us more about those experiences to enable us to have what it takes to help other people that God will bring into our lives who may be going through what we have experienced.

The life of Joseph in the book of Genesis is a perfect example. His own blood brothers mistreated him; they sold him into slavery to strange people who, in turn, sold him to Potiphar. At Potiphar's house, he was falsely accused by the wife of Potiphar and as a result, he was arrested for something that he did not do. Joseph had every right to be bitter because of the unfair treatment, especially by his own brothers, but throughout the account of Joseph, there is no part which reflects that Joseph became bitter. We know the end of the story of Joseph, that God promoted him to be the governor of the whole of Egypt, and at a certain time, his brothers came to seek help and it was Joseph who welcomed them. Just notice that Joseph was never bitter with them but he said the words in the scripture below:

20. 'But as for you, you thought evil against me; but God meant it for good, to bring to pass, as it is this day, to save much people alive.'

– Genesis 50:20(Amplified).

You can see how God used what his brothers meant for evil to push Joseph to his destiny. God always has a bigger picture of our lives. Some of the things that happen in our lives we may not understand. They might be painful, shameful and hurtful but if we can have the attitude of Joseph of not holding bitterness in the inside of us, God is able to make all things work together for good. Joseph went through a difficult time in his life for years, but he never allowed bitterness to take root in his life and, as a result, God uplifted him to a high position in life. Do you realise that what Joseph went through was to prepare him to have the experience for where God was taking him? So it is in your life; what you are going through is not there to kill you or to make you bitter but to prepare you to have what it takes to go where God is taking you to, as long as you do not allow your challenges to make you bitter. Whatever has happened in your life, do not allow bitterness to take root in your life, but always forgive and have the attitudes of Joseph by keeping yourself pure on the inside.

There is no revenge that is as powerful and effective as forgiveness. When you do good to people who have hurt you, you are actually giving them a challenge to change and do things the right way. Always remember that forgiveness is the greatest gift you can give to yourself because forgiveness has little to do with another person as it is an internal issue. I have heard many people, during a counselling session, say 'I can forgive but I cannot forget', but what they do not understand is that they have not forgiven. When you forgive, you should take that offence out of your mind completely, for if it is still there in your mind, the moment you think about it, it will just open those wounds of hurt afresh. True forgiveness should be like a cancelled note that was torn into two pieces and set on fire so that it cannot be shown against anyone again.

Most people today are still living under the law, which said an eye for an eye and tooth for tooth; they forget that they are living under the grace. The law came by one man; Moses. It brought condemnation and bondage to people, but the gift of grace was brought by one man, Jesus Christ the righteous one, so that we can live a free life. I am encouraging you today not to live a life of bondage by allowing the spirit of unforgiveness to take control over your life. Forgive and live a life that Jesus was sacrificed for. Under the grace, Jesus said 'pray for your enemies and love them, so no matter what has happened to you, always forgive and pray for those people who have hurt you, so that they may change'. When you follow what the word of God is saying, it will help you to live a life full of joy, peace and harmony. The spirit of unforgiveness drives many of the conflicts we have, ranging from our families, workplace and the entire world. I like the powerful statement of Mahatma Gandhi who once said, "If we practice an eye for an eye and a tooth for a tooth, soon the whole world will be blind and toothless". Wow! Powerful! This is the problem we have in the entire world; the problem of unforgiveness. Whenever you refuse to forgive by holding onto bitterness and resentment, this can make you live a miserable life. When a person is holding grudges against someone, they are not living a happy life, as most of their life is controlled by the negative emotions they have for the people they are angry with.

Chapter 2.

Understanding the Stages of Bitterness

31. 'Get rid of all bitterness, anger, wrath, clamour, and slander; let it be

Put away from you, along with all malice (all types of evil behaviour).'

– Ephesians 4:31(Amplified).

The scripture above clearly states bitterness first, followed by anger, wrath, clamour and malice. Bitterness is the common denominator of anger, wrath, clamour and malice. These are listed in order of their manifestation or stages, and I will explain each stage by highlighting why and how each stage affects the other if there are not dealt with properly. Wrath, anger, clamour and malice are the fruits of bitterness. I do call them the brothers, sisters and cousins of bitterness, because their roots and strength are from bitterness.

In the previous chapter, I explained that bitterness is an evil attitude which refuses to forgive or to be forgiven. Usually, it manifests itself in sharpness, spitefulness and resentment and as a result of this bitterness, it closes all doors to reconciliation. We then have anger, which is a disposition, which is used to express our displeasure with something that has happened to us. One main thing we should understand is that anger is a normal and a good emotion whose purpose is to push us to deal with something very quickly. When we hold on too long to anger, anger then becomes a weapon and develops to the next stage, which is wrath.

> 26. 'And "don't sin by letting anger control you." Do not let the sun go down while you are still angry.
>
> 27. For anger gives a foothold to the devil.'

– Ephesians 4:26, 27(NLT).

When anger is not dealt with, it gives a mighty foothold to the devil. As the scripture above explains, we must not allow the sun to go down while we are still angry. In other words, it means do not sleep on the issues or go into the next day with yesterday's issues unresolved. The main purpose of anger is to help you deal with things that do not make you happy immediately, so in order to avoid anger developing to the next stage, it is better to quickly deal with what displeases you and let it go before the enemy finds a way in your life. No matter what has happened to you, do not keep or bottle things up on the inside of you; the best thing is to let it go before the enemy uses it as a weapon to destroy your life and peace. When anger is not dealt with, it develops into wrath, which is a point when a person has volatile anger that erupts like a volcano. When you start experiencing this sort of behaviour in your life, you must know that there are times when you have allowed the sun to go down without dealing with them, and now they are starting to manifest themselves in an eruptive volcanic state. When wrath is not dealt with, it also develops to clamour which is a state when a person starts to speak raging words or evil words with the intention of causing harm to the other person. These words can be in the form of shouting, speaking loudly, boasting, or quarrelling. When clamour manifests itself, there is no room for kindness; no matter what words are spoken, the intention is to cause more harm than good. When you are upset you see yourself using harsh words, screaming, shouting and using the words as a method of causing pain or harm to the other person; you must understand that bitterness has taken root in your life. When clamour is not dealt with, it will develop into malice, which is the final act, carried out to injure someone. This is when you see a person killing someone or you see people fighting physically or having an ill will, with the intention of injuring someone.

The Bible rightfully says we must not let the sun go down while we are still angry, but most of the time, we tend to ignore the wise words of God in the Bible and, as a result, we go through situations that ruin our life and future. Forgiveness is always a hard thing do for most people in the world, although it is the right thing to do to keep you happy, leading a successful life that is stress-free and full of joy. I want to highlight some of the causes of bitterness, how you can overcome them and how you can set yourself free from the bondage and imprisonment of unforgiveness. The seed of bitterness is originally an offence and the offence can be anything ranging from an event, a word, a comment or facial expression that offended you. There are so many forms or causes of bitterness; it may be when someone has cheated on you, losing your marriage or going through a divorce, being abused as a child, or when someone has belittled you, or maybe you have been betrayed by someone you trusted so much. There are so many causes of bitterness or offence that the list is endless but, no matter what form of offence you have experienced in your life, please do not allow bitterness to take root in your life. The painful things you may have gone through in life may qualify you naturally to be bitter or angry, but as a child of God, the Bible teaches us to forgive our enemies and all those who have offended us.

Unforgiveness blocks our prayers from being answered, and when you are bitter with someone who has offended you, the very person who is suffering the most is you, not the opposite. Usually, the people or the person you are holding the grudge or the offence against, wherever there are, are enjoying their lives and some of them are not even aware that they have offended you. Some of them do not mind about how you feel, so why do you allow people who do not care about you to control your life? Whenever you are bitter about someone, always know that you are allowing that person to live in your mind rent-free, so when you forgive you are actually doing yourself a great favour. Sometimes, you may find it difficult to forgive someone because they did not apologise or show any remorse. Yes, they might have shown those attitudes to you but remember that forgiveness has nothing to do with what the other person is feeling, but it depends entirely on you. Whether people apologise or not, your responsibility is to forgive and set yourself free from the bondage of bitterness because, when you are holding onto bitterness and unforgiveness, you are the very person who is suffering the most. If anyone has hurt you before, why do you allow them to continue to hurt you year after year in your mind? Forgive and set yourself free from the self-made prison wherein you are both the prisoner and the jailer. When you take a step to forgiving everyone who has hurt you, you will discover that you have set yourself free from the self-made prison. When you forgive, you will also realise that you have released all the pain and the hurt that people have caused you and that will cause you to experience the peace and joy that surpasses all understanding.

When you hold onto bitterness and resentment for a long time, the roots of bitterness will grow deeper and make it more difficult to forgive. The Bible tells us to be quick to forgive and to be slow to anger and the reason for this is that when we hold resentment towards someone, we are literally bound or a slave to that person by an emotional link that is stronger than steel. When you forgive, you are disconnecting yourself from the link and taking control of your life. The researchers have also shown that there are serious mental, emotional and physical consequences that affect people who have an unforgiving heart. Unforgiveness is linked to a lessening of chronic back pain and depression and, in other people, it reduces the level of stress hormones. Unforgiveness can turn your immune system inside out and as a result, it makes you more prone to diseases. The discovery of this research shows how important it is for us to forgive, and it is all for our benefit, not those against whom we are holding grudges.

Part 2.
How Do I Get Out of the Cycle of Bitterness?

Chapter 3.

Breaking the Bitterness Cycle

Bitterness is usual nurtured when one takes secret delight in plotting revenge and the strength of the root of bitterness depends on how long it has been nurtured. As I said before, the longer you take to forgive, the harder it becomes to let it go, and this will cause you to live a dismal life at best. God created us to live a life full of joy, peace and love but when we are bottling up bitterness and resentment, we are robbing ourselves of the life that God has intended us to live. The other important factor if you want to break out of the cycle of bitterness and resentment, is to be able to identify the root causes of your bitterness and be able to uproot them or deal with them completely. I stated in a previous chapter that the root cause of unforgiveness is bitterness which is the refusal to forgive and to be forgiven, so you need to discover what has caused you to be bitter. When you can identify the causes of it, then you will be in a position to be able to deal with them.

A tree has roots and branches, and the roots give life to the rest of the tree, which include the branches that carry the fruits. You may take away all the leaves and fruits from the tree without uprooting its roots, and the tree will produce other leaves and fruits again, but if you pull up the roots, the tree will completely die and cease to exist. The same principle applies in forgiveness; if you try to work on things like anger, wrath, clamour, and malice, and you do not deal with the root cause of them which is bitterness, you will not break out of the cycle of bitterness. As I have stated in the previous chapter, bitterness is nurtured by taking secret delight in plotting revenge, and the best way of breaking out is by exposing and destroying the root causes. The root causes of bitterness are also the result of not dealing with the hurt and challenges in the correct way. Let the negative thoughts of delighting in plotting revenge go out of your mind, and programme your mind with the word of God, then that will give you victory over bitterness. You need to accept that you are hurt, but at the same time, you need to understand that forgiveness is for your own benefit, not for the person who has hurt you. We need to understand that things that happen in life will make us either better or bitter; at the end of the day, the choice is ours. As a Christian, always choose to see things differently, based on what the word of God says about you.

Steps of Getting Out of the Cycle of Bitterness

1. Let God Fight Your Battles

19. 'Never take your own revenge, beloved, leave room for the wrath of God, for it is written, "VENGEANCE IS MINE, I WILL REPAY," says the Lord.'

– Romans 12:19 (NAS).

Knowing that God is in control in our lives and is going to revenge on our behalf will help us to let go of anything that has hurt us. By doing this, we will able to come out of the cycle of bitterness. This is usually a big challenge for most people because they want to deal with the people who have hurt them personally and directly. This method of revenge usually creates more challenges and worsens the situation but leaving everything to God will be the best solution as it will execute the right and appropriate revenge for you. Knowing that God knows everything that has happened to you will always give you the assurance that nothing will go unnoticed and be unaccounted. Walking in bitterness will only rob you of the joy and love that is at your disposal, because of what God has done for you through His son Jesus Christ. God wants you to live a life full of joy, peace and love. The definition of our God is love as He showed it by sending His son Jesus Christ. Having an understanding that their nature is love that is unconditional, will make you realise that you need to get rid of the unforgiveness and bitterness as this is not in the nature or DNA of our heavenly father. Choosing to walk in love and developing positive thoughts and the right mindset that is influenced by what the word of God is saying about your attitude towards offence or bitterness will play a vital role in getting out of the cycle of bitterness.

2. Focus on the Positives

8. 'Finally, brethren, whatsoever things are true, whatsoever things are honest, whatsoever things are just, whatsoever things are pure, whatsoever things are lovely, whatsoever things are of good report; if there be any virtue and there be any praise, think on these things'.

– Philippians 4:8 (KJ)

The other most important thing to break out of the cycle of bitterness is to think positive as the scripture above is advising us to do. The mind is the forerunner of everything; if our mindsets are programmed with positive thoughts, so shall our lives be. Remember this principle that our thoughts become words, our words determine our actions, our actions become our habits, our habits become our character and our character finally shapes the course of our destiny. Opting to focus on positive things that have happened or are happening in your life will help you to shift your attention from the negative energy that fertilises bitterness and channel it to the positive energy that will help you to move forward successfully. Always remember that we have the DNA of our heavenly father, which is love, therefore, we are created to express love to others and, at the same time, live a joyful happy life.

7. *'For as he thinks in his heart, so is he.'*

– Proverbs 23:7 (Amplified).

The scripture tells us that as the person thinks, so is he, meaning that the direction of your actions is determined by what is in your mind, which, in turn, means that you will never rise above your thinking mentality. This means that you cannot be living in the cycle of bitterness and yet you wonder why you are not happy and enjoying life. The mind is like a computer; a computer has software that is programmed to determine how it is going to work. What you programme into that software of the computer will determine how it is going to work. The same principle applies to our minds; our lives will always go in the direction of what is programmed in our minds. Therefore, programming our minds with positive thoughts will help us to come out of the cycle of bitterness, to live a life of victory.

3. Choose to be Better, not Bitter

God has blessed everyone with the power of choice, and He has given us his word, which contains the truth that will set us free. When one is trapped in the cycle of bitterness, you are actually a slave to bitterness and to those people who have made you bitter, and those people are actually your bosses, determining what life you are supposed to live. There is nothing that happened to you that is a surprise to God. The pain, the agony, shame, betrayal, and all sorts of negative things that have happened to you, God knows about them. In Romans 8: 28, God's word tells us that all things work together for good for those who are called for His purpose. All things working together for good means the good things and the bad things all work together for good, so at the end of that pain, that challenge, all things will work together for good. You just need to keep the right attitude and obey what the word of God is saying concerning forgiveness. When you come to an understanding that God created you on purpose for a purpose, then you realise that you are very important in the eyes of God and He will never allow whatever you are going through to pull you down and make you bitter. This is the time to reprogram your mental computer with the right thoughts bearing in mind that you are special, unique, wonderful and fearfully created by God to live a life full of joy, peace and love. The bitterness will always rob you of becoming who God created you to be and rob you of living your life to the full potential.

> *20. 'But if your enemy is hungry, feed him and if he is thirsty, give him a drink, for in so doing you will heap burning coal on his head.*
>
> *21. Do not be overcome by evil but overcome evil with good.'*

– Romans 12:20-21(NIV).

The best way of revenging those who have hurt you is to do good to them, as the scripture above also supports this statement. One thing I have learnt through the experiences of life is that there are people with PHDS- meaning Pull Him/Her Down Syndrome, and these are people who will do anything in their power to offend and pull you down. When you allow them, they will make you bitter and pull you into their arena of negativity, rage, bitterness, and fighting and then beat you with experience, then you will be down and out forever. Do not allow people with negative attitudes or low self-esteem to pull you to their level of bitterness but remember that you are better than that; you are destined to fly high like an eagle.

The eagle does not associate itself with chickens, because they cannot fly, but an eagle can fly about 15000ft above the ground. The most amazing thing about the eagle is that it can feed on dangerous snakes, but it picks the snake from the ground, which is its territory, and carries it to a high altitude in the air to a point where the snake cannot breathe. The snake will be having no stamina to fight back, so at that point, it will drop the snake down but before it reaches the ground, it will take it up again to a high attitude until the snake is dead. When the snake is dead, the eagle will then come down and feed on a good meal of snake. If the eagle had tried to kill the snake on the ground, which is its territory, the snake could have easily killed the eagle. My point is, do not allow negative, critical, judgemental, cynical and below-par people to pull you into their level, but be the one who pulls them to your level. The level that you are at as a Christian is that of walking in love, doing good to those who have hurt you by not allowing bitterness to take root in your life. When you practice Bible principles, they will make you a better person rather than being a bitter person. The other fascinating thing about the eagle is that it has an enemy called the crow; whenever it sees the eagle it will fight it. There is one amazing thing that the eagle does; it flies to an altitude where the crow cannot breathe, and the crow will not have an option but to back off from fighting the eagle. As we all know, the eagle is the king of the birds, and the crow is a very small bird compared to the eagle, which means that an eagle can easily fight back the crow, but the eagle chooses to end what is supposed to be a fight in a peaceful manner by avoiding the crow. This is exactly what the Bible is encouraging us to do; we must always strive for peace by walking in love and not allowing the sun to go down while we are still angry, the end result of which is bitterness.

4. Choose to Walk in Love

4. Love is patient, love is kind, it does not envy, it does not boast, it is not proud.

5. It is not rude, it is not self-seeking, it is not easily angered, it keeps no record of the wrongs.

6. Love does not delight in evil but it rejoices with the truth.

7. It always protects, always trusts, always hopes, always perseveres.

8. 'Love never fails....'

13. 'And now these three remain: Faith, Hope and Love. But the greatest is Love.'

– 1 Corinthians 13: 4-8, 13. (NIV)

Walking in love is the greatest thing to do in order to get out of the cycle of bitterness. The scripture clearly states the fundamental attributes of love, and walking by putting into practice what the word of God is saying will make you live a free and victorious life. Some of the qualities of love are that 'it is not easily angered, it keeps no records of the wrongs'. As Christians, we are required to walk according to what the word of God is requiring us to do. When we learn not to keep any records of the wrongdoings of others, this will help you to break away from the cycle of bitterness and unforgiveness. Walking in love is the best way that will help you to live a life full of joy, peace, love and live the life that God has created for you to enjoy. The most common weakness that most people have is that they are more led by their emotions rather than what the word of God tells them to do. Know the truth and the truth shall set you free; knowing the truth and abiding in the truth of God's word will bring liberty in your life and break every chain of bitterness and unforgiveness in your life. The definition of God is love and that is why He sent His only beloved son to die for us and redeem us from the oppression of the devil and his agent. He loves us unconditionally. When you were born again, you inherited the DNA of your heavenly father, which is the DNA of love, therefore if you are a mature Christian who is called by His name, so walking in love should be your daily lifestyle.

19. 'We love because He first loved us.'

– 1 John 4:19 (NIV).

God has set an example for us to follow. Sometimes, things that happen to us are so painful and hard to bear, but we need to stand on the principle of God's word and, if we do so, God will give us the strength to move on in life.

We must not forget that we have the person of the Holy Spirit inside of us to help us during our weakness and in the areas where we are struggling. The Holy Spirit is our helper in times of need; relying on the Holy Spirit when you are weak or struggling with something will cause you to be victorious. Living a life of walking in love will allow you to experience the joy that God has intended for you. Psychology also tells us that if we are to live a balanced life that is healthy, we must learn to love others in order to be loved. When you look around in your community, workplace and family, you will discover that most of their failures are as a result of not loving, because when you experience the reality of someone's love, that tends to help you to be able to love yourself and others. When you learn to forgive and walk in love, it will help you to live a peaceful life. Most divorces that are happening can be minimised and there will be more unity and peace in families, communities, workplaces and in the whole world.

Chapter 4.

Letting Go of the Past

The greatest challenge we have in life is to let go of the past and this results in unforgiveness, resentment, bitterness and self-blame situations. We often forget to take into consideration that we cannot change our past. The past is history and we need to only take the positive lessons that we have learnt from it. Letting go of the past includes letting go of the emotional wounds, hurt, disappointment and mistakes that you have made that cost you a lot of things. I believe there are four stages in the life span of every person, which are:

1. Hindsight

Hindsight is from the word behind. Most people are so tied up to their past they cannot let it go, and everything that is negative that has happened in their past is still so much part of their lives. One thing they forget is that you cannot move forward while you are holding onto your past; clinging to your past is a recipe for disaster and, at the same time, it causes stagnation in your life. Something that we need to know is that an iron that is not used will rust, and stagnant water stinks. When you stay holding onto your past or hindsight, it will stop you from moving forward to achieve your dreams. Let your past be for inspiration not for limitation. Many people are stuck in the cocoons of the past, living a life of regret and pointing fingers at themselves and others because of their past failures and disappointments. Living a life of hindsight is like driving a car in reverse; you definitely know that you are not going to go very far and the chances of falling in the ditch are high. When you look at the car, the rear-view mirrors and the side mirrors are all very small, compared to the front windscreen and the reason why the front windscreen is big is because it is more important where you are going to, than where you are coming from. Let go of the past; your future is bigger and brighter than your yesteryears. There is no reason for hanging onto the past while there is so much at stake ahead of you. Let go of your past glories and past failures. You can briefly look back on your past to remind yourself of the victories that God has given you, but do not allow your past glories or disappointments to dominate your present life. I have met people in my life who are stagnant in their lives and are not moving forward because they are always talking about their past achievements. Some are dwelling on their past failures and disappointments and they are not being fruitful in their present life.

2. The Insight

Insight is your dreams, your aspirations, what God has deposited in the inside of you, or things that you want to fulfil in your life. God has created each one of us on purpose for a purpose, so each one of us has goals to accomplish. Letting go of the past means not focusing much on your past, and starting to focus on your insight.

3. The foresight

When you are aware of your insight, the next thing is the foresight. This involves an immediate plan of what you want to achieve this year and the coming year, and these are short-term goals. Planning and setting goals you want to achieve in the year you are in and the next year or so will help you to stop focusing on the past.

4. The farsight

The farsight is developed from the foresight. The farsight is the road map to indicate where you want to be in 5 years, 15 years, and 30 years and so on. This is long-term planning that will help you to keep going and be focused on the future, not on your hindsight. The main purpose of these sights is to help you to move forward with a clear direction and at the same time having something to look forward to achieving.

12. 'Not that I have already obtained all this or have already been made perfect, but I press on to hold that for which Christ Jesus took hold of me.

13. Brothers, I do not consider myself yet to have taken hold of it. But one thing I do: Forgetting what is behind and straining towards what is ahead.

14. I press on towards the goal to win the prize, for which God has called me heavenward in Christ Jesus.'

– Philippians 3:12-14 (NIV).

Letting go of the past is the best thing to do if you want to achieve your insight, foresight and farsight. Paul is a good example for us to follow; he did not have a good history in life but when he experienced the Damascus transformation, his life changed forever. Paul clearly knew that his past was very bad; remember, this is the very person who was called Saul who persecuted the church of God, killed and arrested many Christians. When Stephen was killed, the Bible says they killed Stephen and they laid the garments of Stephen at the feet of a young man called Saul. When we summarise everything, Paul was a killer and a persecutor of the church but after his Damascus transformation, he decided to let go of his negative past and focus on where he was going or on his call.

Paul clearly states in the verses above that one thing he does is forget things that are behind and press ahead to the prize which God has called him to do. Paul became one of the greatest apostles in the history of the Bible, highly anointed, established many churches and wrote most of the books in the New Testament. What made Paul so successful in his calling was letting go of his past and focusing on where he was going.

The life of Paul is quite an inspiration to all of us to learn to let go of the past and understand that our past does not determine our future; God does determine our future if we can decide to let go of our past. I just want to encourage you, as you are reading this book, to let go of the past. God has greater and bigger plans for your life, and your past is nothing compared to what is ahead of you. You are destined for greatness, you are a king or a Queen in the eyes of the Lord, and your best days are ahead of you, not behind you. What may look like a setback in your life is actually not a setback but a set-up for your great comeback. What looked like a stumbling block is going to be converted into a stepping stone to where you are going.

The other perfect example in the Bible is the example of King David who committed murder and adultery but never allowed his past mistakes to keep him from getting closer to God. God even said David is a man after my own heart. David followed the principle of letting go of the past; he knew that he could not change his past but he could change his present and his future. Living a life of past regrets, bitterness and unforgiveness will always be the biggest setback of your life. If you look around the world, greater people who are successful and have achieved a lot, they are people who have experienced difficult things in their lives, but they decided to let go of bitterness and hold on to their hindsight. They understand one principle; that their experience was for making them better and not bitter. I always believe that extraordinary people with an extraordinary destiny will always go through extraordinary challenges but the good thing is that they save an extraordinary God. The experiences are not a setback but a set-up to make you more effective, wiser and have the experience to accomplish your destiny. Most of the things you have gone through were simply a ministry in the making. The things that made most people or you bitter are the very things that God is going to use to make you shine, becoming great and unstoppable. God starts from chaos to cosmos, which means that God can use your messy past life to bring something great and fruitful out of it.

God wants us to let go of the past and to focus on the future that is greater and brighter, so do not let bitterness and unforgiveness take root and become a setback in your life. God knows about all the good and the negative things that have happened in the past. He will certainly make them work together for your own good. This is the time and the season to let go of the past and press on towards the bright future that is ahead of you, as your future is better than your past. People may have hurt you; just let it go. Life has treated you unfairly; just let it go. You may have been betrayed by the people you trust; just let it go. You may have made dreadful mistakes that have caused you to be bitter; just let it go. God can turn your Mess to a Message. God can turn your Scars to Stars. God can turn your Disappointment to Re-appointments. God can turn your Test to Testimonies, and God can turn your Trials to Triumph. God can turn your Misery to Ministry, God can move you from being a Victim to a Victor and God can move you from being the tail to being the head, therefore, do not let bitterness take root in your life. This is the time to let go of the past. There is no need to hold onto the past if you have a revelation that all things work together for good and your future is more glorious. This is the time for you to forgive all the people and the things that have caused you to be bitter in your past. This is the time to move on knowing that God is fighting your battle and He will bring justice to those who have treated you unfairly.

Declarations

- I declare and decree that what looked like a setback in my life was actually a set-up for my great comeback.

- I declare and decree that my stumbling blocks of yesterday were converted into stepping-stones for me today.

- I declare and decree that my trials are unique steps to my sure promotion.

- I declare and decree that I have a clear vision for my destiny and future.

- I declare and decree that the eyes of my understanding are enlightened towards the express will of God for me; therefore, I am not going to hold onto my past.

- I declare and decree that I am lifted above shame and regret in my life, therefore, bitterness and unforgiveness have no room in my life.

- I declare and decree that my today shall be more glorious than my yesteryears.

- I declare and decree that all my breakdowns of the past are being converted to breakthroughs by the power of the Holy Spirit.

- I declare and decree that the time for weeping is over and my new dawn of favour is now.

- I declare and decree that I am like a tree planted by the river and I produce the fruit in season. I am unmovable, unshakable, untouchable and unstoppable because I know who I am in Christ.

Chapter 5.
Your Opposition Determines the Level of Your Greatness

The reason why the enemy is fighting you is that he can see your greatness and how you are going to tear his kingdom down. The people around you are usually the very people that the enemy uses to pull you down. Remember that a stranger cannot do you much harm, but the people who know you are the people who will hurt you the most. When you look at your life today, you will realise that the deepest wounds in your heart were caused by the people around you or closest to you. This is the time to let go of any emotional wounds and remember that you are more than a conqueror, destined for greatness; born to win, fearfully and wonderfully made by God to make a great impact in this world. This is the time to look in the mirror and tell yourself that you are a victor, not a victim, you are the head, not the tail, born to succeed.

The time to let go of the past is now. This is the moment to shake off all bitterness and unforgiveness in your life and strive to fulfil what is ahead of you.

'God says "I know the plans that I have for you, they are not the plans of evil but the plans to give you a future and hope".'

– (Jeremiah 29:11) (NIV).

What is ahead of you is greater than what is behind you. Let go of the past; God has great plans for you, so stop crying for the closed doors, stop focusing on what did not go right in your life and focus on the new opening doors that are bigger and better than your past. Always remember that what is ahead of you is greater than what is behind, and once you have an understanding of this, you will realise that there is no need to cling onto the past emotional wounds. What you went through was not there to destroy you but to prepare you for what is ahead of you, especially if you are a person of destiny. All you have gone through was simply to give you experience that you need for where you are going to.

When the farmer goes out to the fields to sow seeds, he will dig the ground and put the seed down, then cover it with soil. The person who does not understand farming can say the farmer is burying seeds, but the farmer knows that he is not burying the seeds but planting them. The seed may be covered by the soil, in the darkest part of the earth, but the amazing thing is that the very soil that is covering the seed creates a good environment for the seed to germinate and grow and produce many more seeds or fruits. The same principle applies to our lives; we may look like our situations and negative things that people have done to us have buried us; some are our own mistakes, but they happened to make us better. Always remember that you were not buried but planted so that you can be more fruitful and have what it takes to be effective in your life. When you learn to let go of the past, you will realise that the storms and the winds that you faced in your life were not there to destroy you but to push you to your destiny. Letting go of the past is not only about forgetting the past but it involves learning from it and moving on, and it is about making good choices to allow your past to strengthen you rather than strangling you. I encourage you to choose to be better, not bitter, as forgiveness is an attribute for the strong not for the weak. When you forgive, it is not an indication of weakness but of strength and understanding that forgiveness benefits you more than anyone else. When you forgive, you will realise that you were in a self-made prison wherein you were both the prisoner and the jailer, therefore, forgiveness and letting go of the past is a great step of releasing you from the self-made prison to your freedom. Most people do not realise that unforgiveness and not letting go of the past is like drinking a poisonous substance and expecting your enemies to die. The fact is that the impact of the poison will affect you, not the people you are holding grudges against. Why do you not choose to live a free life today, which is full of joy, peace, and free from strife in order to see the best of you?

Living a free life with no strife will make you realise your great potential and the great opportunities that are right in front of you. The other fact is that you cannot drive along the roads of life without sometimes hitting the bumps, such as disappointments, betrayal, regrets, and tragedies of losing the beloved people around you or when you have been cheated on by people you trust so much. When we experience such things in life, they can cause us to be stuck in one place, like someone trying to drive a car looking at the rear-view mirror. You may have bumped into the bumps of road called life, but do not drive your car in reverse; instead, focus on where you are going to by driving using your forward gears and looking through your front windscreen which will make your driving easy.

Living a life of holding onto the past will keep you in one place and rob you of fulfilling your destiny, so choose today to focus on your foresight and farsight by letting go of the past. Remember that you cannot reach what is in front of you unless you let go of what is behind you. This is the time, as you are reading this chapter, to let go of the past and apprehend or pursue what is in front of you.

There is a need for every one of us to understand that everything we experience in life is not to benefit us only, but through our experiences, we can be able to encourage others. As a child of God, you will realise that what you have gone through will determine your grace and anointing in certain areas of your life; in other words, what you have gone through was simple a ministry in the making. The sincere truth is that you cannot lead people effectively to a place or level you have never been, so what you have gone through in life was a necessity to give you enough experience to face your future endeavours and assignments.

The perfect biblical example of why God sometimes allows us to go through challenges is the life of Moses. He was raised in Pharaoh's house and exposed to a high level of education and living a glamorous life in a royal palace. The reason why Moses was born was to deliver the children of Israel from slavery in Egypt; that was the reason why God protected him. God allowed him to grow up, and to be protected in the palace while other male babies were killed. Moses had all the skills and the expertise of the Egyptians, for as you know, Egypt was a civilised nation already by then. Moses knew that he was born to deliver the Israelites from slavery, but he tried to deliver a solitary Israelite at the wrong time. It was not God's timing and he had to wait for God's timing. Moses was doing the right assignment at the wrong time and it became a wrong thing because God knew that Moses was not yet ready to deliver His people. He did not have the experience and knowledge to execute God's mission for his people.

When we look at the life of Moses from a natural eye, we may assume that it was going to be easy for God to tell Moses to tell Pharaoh to let His people go, as Moses was living in the same palace as Pharaoh. The main reason why God did not instruct Moses to do so is that he did not have the wilderness and the leadership experience. God had to use an uncomfortable situation to take Moses out of the comfort zone at the palace to gain wilderness experience. When we follow the account of Moses, we realise that after Moses ran away from the palace, he spent a number of years in the wilderness looking after the flock of his father-in-law. Then God saw that Moses had the necessary experience and it was the right time to lead His people out of captivity. The angel appeared in the burning bush and instructed Moses to start the steps of leading the children of Israel from Egypt to the Promised Land. My main point about the account of Moses is to highlight that what you have gone through was there to prepare you for what is ahead of you. Let go of the past, and do not allow it to make you bitter; it will serve its purpose in your life as you press on towards the goal that is ahead of you. Moses had to go through the preparation to get experience before leading the children of Israel out of slavery, and so it is in your life, God is able to turn your misery to ministry and your mess to a message. Therefore, rise up and wise up; it is a new dawn.

There are sixty-six books in the Bible. You are the sixty-seven book of the Bible. There are people who are not going to read the Bible but they are going to read your life stories, challenges and how you overcame them. The testimonies you will share with them will make them motivated to change. The way in which you overcame your challenges will also make them want to know the God you save. What I have learnt from my life is that you are not required to preach a sermon by opening the Bible every time, but sometimes you just need to share your testimonies of victory that will change many people's lives. Mark 5: 18-20 tells us that after Jesus had cast out the demons from a certain man, He ordered him to go to his hometown and tell them what had happened to his life. When people heard his testimony, they were amazed and they believed. My point is that this man did not have a word or scriptures to share with other people, but his testimony became a powerful message to share in his hometown.

There are times when you need to say, read my story, read my life, the gospel according to me. God allows us to go through certain circumstances so that we can use them to encourage others to overcome their challenges or to know that God is the deliverer. There is no point in being bitter about your past; it will work for your own good and that of others, as the Bible says that all things work together for good. All things here means both the good and the bad things, which will work for your own good as long as you let go of the past, bitterness and unforgiveness by focusing on what is ahead of you. One thing that I have learnt in life is that, it is not always about reaching or fulfilling our destination only, but it is also the things that happen on our way to our destiny that matter the most. The things that happen on our way to our destiny are the ones that prepare us to have what it takes to fulfil our destiny, as I highlighted earlier about the life of Moses.

God mostly teaches us more on our way to our destiny than when we have reached there. For example, when you are into leadership, God will teach you more about your leadership skills prior to having an opportunity to lead. When you come to a point of understanding these principles about life, you will never allow bitterness to take root in your life. You understand that there are things you have to go through in preparation for where you are going. Most of the time it is very hard when you go through those gloomy, dark and traumatic times, but always remind yourself that, on the other side of the clouds, the sun is ever shining. When you learn to let go of your past emotional wounds, God will cause those people who hurt you, and rejected you to reach out for you, this time not to hurt you or reject you, but to reach out for help from you. The same thing happened to Joseph. The same family who were jealous of him to the point that they sold him into slavery thinking that they were destroying his life forever, years later reached out to Joseph, this time not to hurt him but asking for help. This is what usually happens when you learn to keep the right attitude about the things that happened in your life, and always remember that vengeance is not for you but for God.

We are saving the God of 3Rs; God records, remembers and rewards. So, this means, whatever has happened in your life, God has recorded it all, then, when the time is right, He will remember and reward you double with joy and wipe all your tears from your eyes, and give you a reason to smile. There is a saying that says, 'He who laughs last laughs the loudest laugh'; therefore, if you can let go of the past, God will put the loudest laugh in your mouth and that will make people recognise that your story has changed for the better. This is the time to let go of the past by not allowing the regrets or the setbacks of yesterday destroy the hopes and dreams of your tomorrow. Apostle Paul had a terrible past, yet he said, 'one thing I do is let go of what is behind me and focus on what is ahead'. This is the attitude we need to have in order to live a successful life that is rewarding. Paul did not only let go of the past but he went on to write most of the books in the New Testament, so, it is no wonder why, at the end of his life, he said, 'I have fought a good fight of faith and now I am waiting for my crown'.

When God wants to lift you to another level in life, there is always going to be a chosen opponent or adversary that you are supposed to overcome in order to get your promotion. The good biblical example is Moses, in his endeavour to deliver the children of Israel from slavery in Egypt; Moses had a chosen adversary by the name of Pharaoh. Moses had to go past Pharaoh before leading the children of Israel from Egypt, but once he managed to pass him, he then managed to execute his assignment. The same principle applies in our lives. There are things, which are like Pharaoh in our lives that we need to go past before accomplishing our assignment or getting elevated to the next level. This is the time to realise that everything you are going through in life serves a purpose. God may have allowed you to go through sickness so that you can minister healing when He heals you. God may have allowed you to go through chaos so that you can minister peace, or go through abuse so that you can minister about the importance of forgiveness. As a Christian, always remember that not all sermons are spoken; some sermons are situational sermons to teach those who do not read the Bible to know that there is God through your situation. The things that you went through were not in vain, because there are the ones that will determine how high you can go and how effective you become in life. I have discovered in life that people with extraordinary destiny will always go through, or face extraordinary challenges, and the good thing is that they serve an extraordinary God who always gives them extraordinary victory.

Letting go of the past disappointments is the best thing to do to yourself because disappointments may lead to discouragement. The challenge with discouragement is that if you stay too long in it, it becomes a sickness called depression. Depression makes you live a miserable life that will rob you of enjoying what Jesus has made possible for you. Disappointments make you lose faith and start doubting yourself and God, and can also lead to living a life of low self-esteem that will cripple your potential and turn you into seeing yourself as a victim rather than a victor. Let go of the past and open a new page of victory, success, of being a winner, an overcomer and a victor, not a victim.

16. 'The Lord said to Samuel, "How long will you mourn for Saul, since I have rejected him as king over Israel? Fill your horn with oil and be on your way; I am sending you to Jess of Bethlehem. I have chosen one of his sons to be king"'.

– 1 Samuel 16:1 (NIV).

Samuel is a good example of people who do not want to let go of the past easily. Samuel took a long time raising Saul to be the first king of Israel, so there were, of course, bonds between them that developed over the years. When God had rejected King Saul, Samuel found it very difficult to let go of King Saul despite God's disapproval of him until it prompted God's reaction on the issue. We know the story; God finally told Samuel to go to the house of Jess to anoint the new King that He had chosen. Cutting the story short, Samuel went there and anointed David who became the greatest king in the account of the Bible. The point is that if Samuel had carried on mourning for King Saul, he could have missed anointing David who later became the greatest King. Today, most people are still suffering from the Samuel syndrome of not wanting to let go of the past, as we are afraid or uncomfortable to venture into new territories or in trying new things. When you do not let go of the past you will miss out on better things that lie ahead of you. Why do you not let go of the past now and step into something bigger and better? This is the time to let go of Saul, for the new King David is waiting for you. Let go of your past regrets, disappointment, hurt, betrayal, and emotional wounds and step into new bigger doors that are ahead of you.

Chapter 6.

My Traumatic Life as a Child and How I Let Go of Bitterness

The main reason to write briefly about my life is to inspire you, not for sympathy. I have gained so much inspiration from my past traumatic life and it has helped me to achieve a lot in life, and to change so many lives around the world. I hope that, as you read my journey of life, you will be inspired and realise that with God all things are possible; it does not matter what you have gone through, God is able to turn your mess to a message and your misery to ministry. My traumatic life as a child has turned out to be a powerful ministry and a powerful message that has opened many doors for me around the world in inspiring others who are experiencing challenging times in their lives. The things that the devil meant for evil, embarrassment and destruction in my life, God turned them to work together for good, and, at the same time, it has determined the anointing and grace upon my life.

I was the middle child in a family of seven, which means three before me and three after me, and this was a middle-class family. When I was between seven and eight years old, I discovered that I was not treated the same as my other siblings. We grew up on farms or rural areas. My dad would go to the major city to do some shopping for clothes twice or three times a year. One day, my father travelled to the city to do shopping for clothes for the whole family, and to my surprise when he came back, he had bought clothes for everyone except me. When I asked Where my clothes were, I was told that my father lost some money before he actually bought my clothes, hence the reason why he did not buy clothes for me. This was the beginning of my miserable and traumatic life; this became a norm and a lifestyle that I was supposed to cope with for the rest of my childhood. My father began to be very abusive towards me and abused me emotionally, verbally and physically, saying things like, 'you are stupid', 'you will not amount to anything'. I went through a lot of peer pressure at school as other children could notice that I was not dressed like my other siblings, and most of the time, I did not have decent clothes, sometimes walking bare-footed compared to my siblings. I became a stranger in my own family's home and the rest of my older siblings joined in and showed me attitude and treated me different. I never experienced parental love in my childhood life; I tried to commit suicide three times because of loneliness and rejection from my own family, the peer pressure from school and the community. I developed the spirit of fear for my father, because, just for nothing, I would be seriously beaten and called all sort of negative words and this caused me to develop low self-esteem, anger and bitterness.

When it came time to go to secondary school, I was sent to a school that did not have enough classes, books and teachers to study, while my other siblings were studying in towns and boarding schools with a good standard of education and facilities. The secondary school I attended was about thirty-two miles from home, so I had to stay there from Sunday evening to Friday, then on Friday, I had to walk home through the bushy roads at night, where there were all sorts of dangerous snakes and other dangerous creatures, to get home between 22:00 to midnight. I used to eat once a day when I was at school. I used to eat around 22:00 pm and I would not eat again until the following day at the same time because of the limitation of the food I had. When the weekend was over on Sunday, I would again walk thirty-two miles to the place where I was attending my secondary school. When I was in my second year in secondary, I came to a point of quitting on focusing on the negative things that were happening in my life and started to focus on the future and how to achieve my dreams. The greatest step I took was to forgive my family for the treatment they were showing me and I started to work on developing high self-esteem about my life. I started to counterattack every negative word that was pronounced in my life with positive ones, and I started to think of how I could possibly advance my life and how I could have a bright future.

When I was walking these thirty-two miles on Friday, going to my parents' home, and on Sunday, back to my secondary place, I used to sing songs to motivate myself and discharge the inner pain that I was going through. As you know, music or singing helps in inner healing and sometimes, I would make positive declarations about my future. Some of the declarations I was making involved praying or talking to God to bless me when I finished school so that I could be a blessing to my family regardless of how they were treating me. God gave me the strength and the grace to finish school, although sometimes, I would go for weeks without attending school because my school fees were not paid and this was not the case with my siblings. Finally, I managed to finish my secondary level, and what happened years after finishing my secondary education was God answering my prayers and wiping my tears from my eyes. When I finished my secondary school, I had to look for a job to be able to sustain myself and to be able to pay for my further studies in order to be competitive in the job market. God began to open doors for me; in short, I studied and became a qualified electrical engineer, then later, I opened a company where I employed more than 15 people and ventured into other businesses. The story of my struggling life changed for the better; God lifted me from glory to glory and later opened doors for me to England where I am permanently based.

When doors opened for me, I became a blessing to my family, especially my parents, as what I used to ask God to do for me actually became a reality. My mother even told my wife that the child they had mistreated had now become the Joseph of this family, referring to the account of Joseph in the Bible. The painful things that my family did to me I repaid by doing good things for them, and remember that the best revenge you can give to people who hurt you, especially your family, is to do good to them. The reason why I wrote briefly about my life is not to expose my family but to encourage you that all things work together for good if you can learn to forgive and have a right attitude in life. I used to walk thirty-two miles in bushy dark roads, exposed to dangerous environments alone, but now, I fly to different parts of the world very often. Flying has become like a hobby to me; remember that this is the very person who used to walk miles and miles but now I am flying around the world. When I was walking all those miles, no one ever knew that I would travel around the world except my God who is the Alpha and the Omega. He is the one who says,

'I know the plans that I have for you; they are not the plans for evil but are the plans to give you a future and hope'.

The very things that looked like a setback when I was a child are the very things that God has used to open many doors for me around the world, preaching about the power of forgiveness and letting go of the past. I have experienced great healings, both emotional and physical, and reconciliation after every meeting that I have held in different parts of the world. I was disadvantaged in my education as a child compared to my siblings but God opened doors for me here in England to study two degrees including a psychology degree and I will be commencing a PhD course in the near future. The things that I went through when I was a child, God has used them to set me up and help those who are struggling in life in the area of forgiveness and abuse. Joseph said to his brothers, what they meant for evil, God has turned it around for good. These are the words that I said to my family, for all the hurtful and negative things they did to me; God has turned them for my good. I am now an ordained pastor, a father, an author, TV personality, visionary and an international speaker but no one saw it coming when I was going through the dark days of my life. The reason I am saying all this is to encourage you to learn to let go of the past for God has better plans for you. He has done it for me, and

God will do it for you as well. This is the time to let go of all negative experiences and focus on what is ahead of you. You cannot afford to continue to drive your car in reverse gear using the rear-view mirrors, because you are not going to go far. Let go of the past now and choose to drive your car with forward gears, using the wider screen in front of you, and enjoy your journey.

Of the things that we encounter on our journey, there are the ones that matter the most because they give us experience and good preparation for where we are going to, as without these tests, we cannot be effective in our destiny, let alone even reaching there. I encourage you today to choose to let go of the past, forgive all those people who hurt you and choose to be happy. I personally went through shame, pain and embarrassment as a vulnerable child, yet I found it necessary to let go. You must always remember that nothing happens by accident, but all things happen for a reason. This include the good things and the bad ones, therefore, having this understanding will help you not to focus on your past. When you are going through a challenging period, you may not understand why you are going through what you are going through, but always know that God has a bigger picture for your life. I did not understand why I was going through the difficult times as a child, but I kept going until a certain point in life when God revealed the purpose of me having to go through those challenges as a child. The scripture says;

5. 'Weeping may endure for a night but joy cometh in the morning.'

– Psalms 30:5b (KJV)

This is the time to encourage yourself in understanding that what happened in the past is now history; you cannot change it but you can change your future based on the decisions you make today. When you choose to let go of the past, you are choosing to have a bright future and opening new doors that were closed because of the past you were holding on to. I am asking you to do what I did, by letting go of the past and God has opened many doors for me to help people who are currently struggling with letting go of the past and unforgiveness. God has opened doors for me in radio stations, in TV and I have had many invitations around the world to share the word of God, including the challenging experiences I encountered as a child, and how I managed to let go of my past.

*13. 'No temptation has overtaken you but
such as is common to man; and God is
faithful, who will not allow you to be tempted
beyond what you are able, but with the
temptation, He will provide the way of escape
also, so that you will be able to endure it.'*

– 1 Corinthians 10:13 (NAS).

As the scripture above explains very clearly, God will never allow us to go through something that we cannot handle, but in every trial that we go through, God will always make a way of escape for us. I tried to commit suicide three times as a child but I failed; this was God protecting me for what He had planned for me, so, whatever I went through, it did not manage to terminate my life because God had already made an escape route for me. This also applies to your life; nothing you have gone through or you are going through will destroy you if God has allowed you to go through it. You will always come through it victorious, being a better, stronger, and wiser person and ready to proceed to the destination that God has intended for you. The most fascinating thing that I have heard as a pastor from people who need counselling are the words, 'I am going through this challenge'. The mere fact that they are going through it, but they are not drowning or sinking down, that is a good sign. I always tell them just to keep on going through it and before they know it, it will be behind them. This is the time to break all the chains of unforgiveness and understand that what you went through did not happen to destroy you but to build you up and prepare you for the good things that are ahead of you, prepared by God.

Chapter 7.

The Spiritual and Psychological Consequences of Unforgiveness

Unforgiveness is the root cause of many problems that people tend to experience in life, both spiritual and psychological; I will outline some of these problems under this topic. I have been a pastor for more than 13 years, doing a lot of counselling and I am a psychology graduate and still advancing my studies in psychology. I hope my experiences and my knowledge will inspire you to see life differently and do the right things that will help you to live your life to its fullest potential.

14. 'For if you forgive people their trespasses (their reckless and willful sins, leaving them, letting them go, and giving up resentment) your heavenly Father will forgive you.

15. But if you do not forgive others their trespasses (their reckless and willful sins, leaving them, letting them go, and giving up resentment), neither will your Father forgive you your trespasses.'

– Mathew 6: 14-16 (Amplified version).

The greatest consequence of unforgiveness is unanswered prayers; the scripture above clearly shows that if we do not forgive others, God does not forgive us either. When you hold onto unforgiveness in your life, therefore, your prayers will not be answered, so we can see that unforgiveness is a hindrance to our prayers being answered. During the time I have been in the ministry, I have met people who believed God would heal them and answer their prayer requests, but to no avail, because they have been holding grudges and are not willing to forgive. The main thing that I have done is to take them through what I call forgiveness therapy where I teach them the importance of forgiving everyone they hold a grudge against. At the very time they come to a point of letting go and forgiving, many experience answered prayers, including healing for some, and at the same time, they have experienced a life full of joy, peace and fulfilment.

> 23. 'So if you are offering a gift at the altar
> and you then remember that your brother has
> any (grievance) against you.
>
> 24. Leave your gift at the altar and go. First
> make peace with your brother and then come
> back and present your gift.'
>
> **– Mathew 5:23-24 (Amplified version).**

The scripture above encourages us to forgive before expecting to have our prayers answered. I have seen many people praying, fasting, declaring and decreeing things but seeing no change in their situation because of the hindrances of unforgiveness. Sometimes before complaining about why your prayers are not answered, first check that you are not harbouring unforgiveness in your heart. The reason why God wants us to make peace before presenting our offering or prayers is that He knows that He is not going to answer our prayers if we are bitter. When we live our lives based on the principles of God's word, we will live a victorious life, a life of peace and joy and become who God intended us to be. The word of God also says in John 8:32 - 'that you shall know the truth and the truth will set you free'; aligning ourselves with the truth of the word of God will make us more than conquerors and realise that God does answer prayers when we come before Him with clean hearts. Let this be the time to forgive and let go of the past in order to live a life with purpose and direction. Unforgiveness will make you to lose the focus of your vision and concentrate on the situations that have hurt you.

Unforgiveness brings in bondage in our lives. It is like being trapped in the jail cell of bitterness, serving someone else's sentence while they are walking free of the crime they have committed. Why do you not take a step today toward setting yourself free from this self-imprisonment and walk away from bitterness and unforgiveness? Remember that unforgiveness is like a silent cancer that will eat you from the inside out. Research has discovered that 7 out of 10 people you meet in the street are angry or bitter people; that constitutes seventy percent. That figure includes many Christians, too, who know the truth of God's word but are failing to live according to its principles and find themselves operating under a closed heaven where their prayers are not answered.

Unforgiveness has some health consequences too. People who do not forgive are highly likely to suffer heart-related diseases and chronic back pain, and unforgiveness turns your immune system inside out and makes you prone to diseases. There is a connection between spirituality and our health; as we forgive, we create chances of boosting our immune system and being healthier. The researchers have also discovered that 61% of cancer patients are struggling with one form of unforgiveness, so this suggests that there are many people trapped under the consequences of unforgiveness. The most common thing for people who do not forgive is stress, so when you are stressed, it affects your digestion, sleeping patterns and affect your skin, hair and fingernails. These are just a few consequences of unforgiveness, which are so destructive in our lives. When you realise the consequences of unforgiveness, you will discover that forgiveness helps you to live a healthier life and you are the one who benefits the most from it. Let this be the time when you let go of the hindsight and focus on the insight, foresight and the farsight and always remember that you cannot reach what is ahead of you until you let go of what is behind you. When you understand that all things work together for good, you will realise that you are not a victim but you have the choice to hold onto your past or let go of it and live a free life.

19. 'Now the deeds of the fresh are evident, which are Immorality, impurity, sensuality,

20. idolatry, sorcery, enmities, strife, jealousy, outburst of anger, disputes, dissensions, factions.

21. Envying, drunkenness, carousing and things like these, of which I forewarn you, just as I have warned you, that those who practice such things will not inherit the kingdom of God.'

– Galatians 5:19-21(NIV)

When you look at the above verses you will find that there are many attributes or components of unforgiveness mentioned as the work of the flesh. From a Christian point of view, if we are still struggling with unforgiveness, we are still walking in the flesh. Studying the word of God will help us to become mature Christians who walk in the Spirit rather than in the flesh, as God has also given us the Holy Spirit to be our helper. When you are struggling with unforgiveness, the Holy Spirit is there to help you to have the ability to let go or to forgive.

Part 3.
What Does the Bible Say About Forgiveness?

Chapter 8.
The Benefits of Forgiveness

The benefits of forgiveness are so many, but among them is living a free life of victory, freedom, joy, peace, high self-esteem and knowing that when you pray God hears your prayers. Another benefit of forgiveness is that it gives you the ability to live a healthy life free from strife, bitterness and stress which affect your immune system by making you vulnerable to diseases. When you want to achieve great things in life, the best thing is to let go of the past emotional wounds and focus on what is ahead of you with a positive attitude. Apostle Paul knew that he had a negative past, which is why he chose to say, 'one thing I do is forget things that are behind me, and press on to the goal that is ahead of me'.

22. 'But the fruit of the spirit is love, joy, peace, patience, kindness, goodness, faithfulness,

23. Gentleness, self-control, against such things there is no law.

24. Now those who belong to Christ Jesus have crucified the flesh with its passion and desires.

25. If we live by the spirit let us also walk by the Spirit.

26. Let us not become boastful, challenging one another, envying one another.'

– Galatians 5:22-26 (NIV).

The scripture above is clearly outlining the benefits of walking in the Spirit, which includes forgiveness, and as you can see, there is nothing about the attributes of unforgiveness that are mentioned in the above scripture. The works of the flesh will always wrestle against the fruits of the Spirit, therefore, as a Christian, you have to take some time and do a self-evaluation of your life to determine if your life reflects the fruit of the Spirit or the works of the flesh. The scripture above also shows us that when we walk in the realm of unforgiveness and bitterness, we are simply manifesting the works of the flesh, therefore, we cannot experience the manifestation of the fruit of the Spirit. The fruits of the Spirit include love, joy and peace and many other good fruits of the Spirit cannot manifest in your life as long as you still walk in the flesh, as you know that the works of the flesh do not work together with the fruit of the Spirit. The choice is yours; you can either choose to walk in the Spirit and produce the fruit of the Spirit or choose to walk in the flesh and produce the works of the flesh. When you compare the works of the flesh and the fruits of the Spirit, you will realise that the works of the flesh have nothing to offer you that is good, but when you focus on the fruit of the Spirit, everything mentioned is there to make your life more joyful and fulfilling. When you choose today to walk in the light of God's word, you will be able to see the manifestation of the fruits of the Spirit in your life, and when that happens, you will live your life to the fullest or live a purpose-driven life.

John 8:32 says 'Know the truth and the truth shall set you free'. Choose today to walk in the light of the truth of God's word and live a victorious life that God has intended for you. Forgiveness also helps you to remove the pain and the grudges in your heart, and that will make you happier by living a life full of love, peace and joy. When your heart is pure, God can find a place in your heart to fill with love, and when you are free from grudges, God can start answering your prayers and doing miracles that will change your life forever. I have been a pastor for over 13 years, and I have seen many people getting breakthroughs, victories, great testimonies and mind-blowing miracles because they decided to forgive and to let go of the past, and as a result, God has shown Himself in their lives like never before. The other thing I have always taught people is that every act of forgiveness and letting go of the past emotional wounds is an act of healing yourself, and doing it regularly will make you feel free and full of joy. Forgiveness therapy is what I call the act of forgiveness, and most people who have gone through this forgiveness therapy have learnt to forgive and let go of the past. All the people that I know who have decided to forgive, have had their lives changed from a life of pain, sorrow, hopelessness, and bitterness to a life of victory, peace, joy and high self-esteem. Some of the benefits of forgiveness are:

- Experiencing joy, peace and love.
- God listens to your prayers
- Improved mental health
- Eradication of stress
- Normal or low blood pressure
- Fewer symptoms of depression
- An improved immune system
- An improved heart health
- An improved self-esteem

There are so many benefits of forgiveness, so, if you choose to forgive, you have everything to gain and nothing to lose. Choose to forgive and live the life that God has intended for you, the life of being more than a conqueror, a life of victory and a life of moving from glory to glory. There is power in your words, therefore, as you make the following declaration, believe that what you are declaring it is happening.

Chapter 9.

Forgiveness Versus Unforgiveness.

When you want to walk in love, you need to forgive, as without forgiveness, there is no walking in love and you cannot walk in love without forgiving others and yourself. When you choose to forgive and walk in love by letting go of resentment, bitterness, malice and unforgiveness, you will begin to experience the peace inside of you that surpasses all understanding. The other important thing you need to understand is that you cannot love if you cannot forgive, therefore forgiveness will help you to focus in life and become a loving person.

9. 'After this manner therefore pray ye: Our Father which art in heaven, Hallowed be thy name.

10. Thy Kingdom come. Thy will be done in earth, as (it is) in heaven.

11 Give us this day our daily bread.

12. And forgive us our debts, as we forgive our debtors.

13. And lead us not into temptation but deliver us from evil: For thine is the kingdom, and the power, and the glory, forever. Amen.'

– Mathew 6:9-13 (KJV).

The Lord's Prayer, which Jesus taught His disciples, also highlights the importance of forgiving others because it is the condition that plays a part in the forgiveness our sins. When you do not forgive, the chances of your prayers being answered and your sins being forgiven is limited.

9. 'Love prospers when a fault is forgiven but dwelling on it separates close friends.'

– Proverbs 17:9 (ESV).

35. 'But love your enemies, do good to them,
and lending to them without expecting to get
anything back, then your reward will be great,
and you will be the sons of the Most High,
because He is kind to the ungrateful and
wicked.'

36. 'Be merciful, just as your father is
merciful.'

– Luke 6:35-36 (KJV).

The nature and the definition of our God is love, and this is what He expects us to be as His children. Jesus emphasised the same thing to His disciples by telling them that, 'people will know that you are my disciples if you love each other'. The standard of measuring the maturity of a Christian is love, therefore, if we still walk in bitterness and unforgiveness, that means we have not reached the level of maturity. When we have reached that level, we will know that unforgiveness hinders our prayers being answered, and we will be aware that bitterness and unforgiveness are all the works of the flesh. When we have reached the level of spiritual maturity, we will understand that all things work together for our good, including both the positive and negative, therefore, there is no need to hold onto bitterness. When we have reached the level of maturity, we realise that vengeance is not for us but for the Lord, therefore, there is no need to hold onto unforgiveness. The true mark of maturity is when somebody hurt you and you try to understand their situation rather than trying to fight them back. The scripture is encouraging us to love our enemies and do well for those who have hurt us without expecting anything by being kind to the ungrateful and wicked, because God Himself loves everybody unconditionally. When we have an understanding that Jehovah is our Father, we will strive to imitate His nature of love and, when do this, we will not have any problem with bitterness and unforgiveness. There will be people in life that will hurt you or do things because they want a reaction from you, but do not react to their toxic plans. By not giving them a reaction when they are desperately seeking for it, that will be a more powerful way to get them away from your life. The best revenge on your enemies is to do good to them, and this is the same principle I used to those people who mistreated me in my life.

10. 'Whoever loves his brother lives in the light and there is nothing in him to make him stumble'

11. 'But the one who hates his brother is in the darkness and does not know where he is going because the darkness has blinded his eyes'.

1 John 2:10-11 (NIV).

7. 'Dear friends, let us love one another, for love comes from God. Everyone who loves has been born of God and knows God.'

12. 'No one has ever seen God, but if we love one another, God lives in us and his love is made complete in us.'

20. 'If anyone says, 'I love God' yet hates his brother, he is a liar. For anyone who does not love his brother, whom he has seen, cannot love God, whom he has not seen.

21. And He has given us this command: Whoever loves God must also love his brother.'

– 1 John 4:7, 12, 20-21 (NIV).

The above two scriptures may sound a bit harsh, but at the same time, they are revealing the plain truth. This is what we are required to do if we say we love God; we are His ambassadors in this world, so people need to see God in our lives. We should reflect the nature of God in us; the verses above are making it plainly clear that if we say we love God, then we should love our brothers. The word brother here is not only limited to your siblings but to anyone who you meet in life, one way or the other. If you know that there are people in your life you hate or you are holding a grudge against them, until you forgive them, and love them, you cannot claim that you love God according to the above verses. The true forgiveness is the best thing that will make you live a happy victorious life and get you closer to God. The true reflecting of His nature is by walking in the truth of the light of His word.

'As God's chosen people, holy and dearly loved, clothe yourselves with compassion, kindness, humility, gentleness and patience. Bear with each other and forgive whatever grievances you may have against one another. Forgive as the Lord forgave you. And over all these virtues put on love, which binds them all together in perfect unity.'

– Colossians 3: 12-14 (NIV).

'Because of his great love for us, God, who is rich in mercy, made us alive with Christ even when we were dead in transgressions; it is by grace you have been saved.'

– Ephesians 2:4-5 (NIV).

The most encouraging aspect of forgiving is that God is asking us to do something that He has demonstrated or done. We were once like lost sheep without a shepherd but, out of His love, He has saved us. We did not deserve to be called His own but out of love, God sent His son Jesus to die for us and redeem us from sin and the dominion of Satan. There are times where we go through challenging situations that leave us with deep emotional wounds and, as a result, we find it hard to let go or forgive. The word clearly states that no matter the situation we may face, we are commanded to walk in love and to love our enemies because God knows that He has the right vengeance for all those people who have hurt us.

5. 'I am the vine; you are the branches. He who abides in Me and I in him, he bears much fruit, for apart from Me, you can do nothing.'

– John 15:5 (NIV).

We are called Christians from the word Christ that means Messiah, the anointed one, which means we have the life of Christ in us. The above verse also shows us the very words that Jesus said that He is the vine and we are the branches, as we all know that the branches get their life from the vine. The life we live should reflect the nature of Christ. Jesus' ministry was characterised by compassion, love and forgiveness, and at a certain point, He said 'forgive them for they do not know what they are doing'. These were people that Jesus raised from the dead, healed and fed when they were hungry, and now they were turning against him. Jesus had to show an act of love regardless of what they were doing to him. This is what the word of God is encouraging us to do; this is the time to forgive all those people who hurt you, let you down, abused you, betrayed you, lied about you and spoiled your name. If there is anyone who you are still holding grudges against, this is the time to call them and tell them that you forgive them, no matter what they did to you.

When asking forgiveness, it does not always mean that you are wrong but that you value your peace more than your ego. When you take this step, you will gradually experience a release in your life that bring peace, and healing, and finally, you completely let go of whatever happened. Forgiveness is an attribute for the strong; the weak cannot forgive, therefore, be a strong person and forgive, then by doing so you will be setting yourself free from self-imprisonment where you are both the jailer and a prisoner. Remember that most of your stress comes from the way you respond, not the way life is sometimes. The best thing is to change how you see things, change your attitude, and look for things that are good in challenging situations. Take the lesson you have learnt and find new opportunities to grow yourself and always work on letting go of all the stress, over-thinking, and worrying and focus on your life with high self-esteem.

When you find yourself struggling with letting go of the past, remind yourself that the past is a place of reference when need be, but not a place of residence. May this be the time to let go of the past and live your life to the fullest without pretending. Love without depending (unconditional love), listen without defending (not too judgemental) and speak without offending (nourishing words). Always remember that you are always responsible for how you act no matter how you feel, and remember that God commands us to love others regardless of what they have done to us. This is undoubtedly one of the challenging things for most of the people, to forgive, but if you are struggling with letting it go, just remind yourself about the benefits of forgiving. When you choose to forgive, you have nothing to lose but everything to gain both spiritually and healthwise, as well as being able to focus on where you are going in life without any setbacks and hindrances.

15. 'See to it that no one fails to obtain the grace of God; that no '"root of bitterness" springs up and cause trouble, and by it many become defiled.'

– Hebrews 12:15 (ESV)

When examining the scriptures, not one gives us any allowance to walk in unforgiveness, no matter what we are going through. The reason is, unforgiveness falls under the works of the flesh that are contrary to the fruits of the Spirit and there is no room for it in our Christian walk with God. Letting go is for your benefit because when you forgive, you get the healing of your emotion and when you choose to let go, you grow as a person. The other most important thing is that holding a grudge does not make you strong, but it makes you bitter and, on the other hand, forgiving does not make you weak, but instead, it sets you free. Choose today to walk in freedom, walk in victory, walk in power and walk in dominion over every past setback, emotional wounds, disappointments, betrayals and abuse. God is on your side, and victory and vengeance from God is assured on your behalf.

Chapter 10.

Living the Life that God Intended for You

God wants you to live a life of victory. Living the life that God has intended for you will take a full understanding of who you are, whose you are, and where you are destined to go, knowing God's plan for your life and what it means to be in God's plan. When you have a clear understanding of your full identity in Christ, then you will live a life of victory and dominion. When you look around the world, you will discover that there are issues of racism, tribalism, xenophobia and many more; this is because of an identity crisis. If you do not fully know who you are, you will always have identity issues with others. You will feel like you need to defend your identity, fight for it, even intimidate others in order to be recognised. When you fully understand who you are, you will walk with confidence without being intimidated by others about who they are, what they have and what they are trying to do to you. As a Christian, you have to understand that you are the child of the most-High God bought by the precious blood of Jesus Christ. That is why you are called a Christian, which is a name derived from Christ.

When you write the word Christian and then take off Ian then you will realise that you are left with the word Christ, which means the Anointed One. The Greek word Christos and the Hebrew word Masiah or Messiah all mean the one who is anointed. Jesus said, 'I am the vine, you are the branches'; as you are the branch, you get the life from the main vine. Having an understanding that you are anointed, that the life of Christ is in you, it will make you understand your identity. The anointing you carry is not for picnics but it is there to give you victory to achieve and live the life that God has intended for you to live. The anointing, in a nutshell, is for service, which means that whatever you want to do, the anointing in you will enable you to do it, and by this, I mean everything that is part of God's plan for your life. As a Christian, you must not suffer from an identity crisis because the word Christian by virtue tells you that you are anointed, therefore, you are not just an ordinary person but you are chosen, anointed, called and you have the DNA of Christ in you.

When Jesus says we are the branches and He is the vine, this describes the very life Jesus lived of hypostatic union, which meant that Jesus was both human and at the same time Divine. The divine life of Christ was about doing extraordinary things; He performed miracles, He walked on water, and He showed love to those who hated Him. The natural side of Him meant that He could get hungry, He got tired, and He could be angry sometimes but He never held grudges, bitterness or unforgiveness. As a Christian, when you come to an understanding that the very nature of Christ is in you, you will begin to walk, live and do the exact things that Jesus did during His earthly life.

The full understanding of your identity in Christ will help you to live a life that is free from bitterness and unforgiveness because you will be aware that it is not your nature as a Christian, neither is it the nature of Jesus Christ. Living the life that God has intended for us needs us to fully understand who we are in Christ and what is required of us in our daily living. The moment when we begin walking in the light of who we are in Christ, we start to live a life of victory, dominion and success. Living a life that is Christ-centred means that we will not struggle with things like bitterness or unforgiveness because forgiveness and walking in love was the nature of Christ, therefore we do not have any excuse for not letting go of the past if we truly know our identity in Christ.

34. 'A new commandment I give you, Jesus told his disciples: Love one another, as I have loved you.

35. So you must love one another; by this everyone will know that you are my disciples, if you love one another.'

– John 13:34-35 (NIV).

If we want to experience the manifestation of the life of Christ in us and be able to live the life that God has intended for us, we need to walk in love. Walking in love enables us to experience the life of Christ working in our lives. If we still harbour things like bitterness, unforgiveness, and not wanting to let go of the past, these things will choke the life of Christ in us. Things like bitterness and unforgiveness act as resistors that limit the flow of the anointing in our lives. The field of electronics has resistors which are used to limit the flow of electrical current in equipment; the more resistors, the less flow of current. This is the same way with our walk with God. If we keep many of the things like bitterness, unforgiveness, malice, strife, wrath, clamour and slander which are not the nature of Christ, we are going to experience less of the power of God in our lives. God wants to see us living our lives to the fullest, which is why He made Jesus Christ to be the main vine and made us the branches so that we can tap into the life of Christ and be able to live a life of victory. Today if you have decided to live the life of victory that God has intended for you, you need to make a decision to let go of the past and choose to walk in love. Choosing to walk in love means uprooting any root causes of bitterness and breaking every chain of unforgiveness and allowing God to direct your steps towards fulfilling your God-ordained destiny.

Maybe you are going through one of these things:

- Brokenness in your heart
- Feeling sad
- Hurt
- Upset
- Feeling Depressed
- Hateful
- Suicidal
- Feel like giving up
- Distressed
- Misunderstood
- Worthless
- Incapable
- Ashamed, uneasy, tense and tearful
- Wronged, crushed and lifeless
- Offended, timid and nervous
- Victimised, tortured and pained
- Stressed and bruised

You might have experienced some of the things on the above list or are currently experiencing them, but never give up; you have the life of Christ in you and the Holy Spirit to give you the strength that you need to overcome. Always remember that the key to walking in happiness and in love is the ability to be able to allow God to change your pain to joy, darkness into light and your sorrow into a blessing. God is able to intervene when you come to a point of deciding to let go of the past, let go of bitterness, unforgiveness and by letting God work in your situation. There is no situation that is above the God we save; with Him all things are possible, and He is able to make all things to work together for good. God has promised us that He will not allow us to go through what we cannot handle, so be assured that what you are going through will not destroy you, as long as you surrender everything to God.

7. 'But we have this treasure in earthen vessels, that the Excellency of the power maybe of God and not of us.

8. We are trouble in every side, yet not in distress; we are perplexed but not in despair;

9. Persecuted but not forsaken; cast down but not destroyed'.

2 Corinthians 4: 7-9 (KJV).

37. 'Yet amid all these things, we are more than conquerors, and gain a surpassing victory through Him who loved us.'

– Romans 8:37 (Amplified version)

The Greek word for victory is NIKAO, which translates as to overcome, which means to gain victory, to prevail and to conquer. The above scriptures are giving us assurance that no matter what we are going through right now, God has already given us victory; we have prevailed, and conquered as well, through Christ Jesus who died for us. Defeat and failure are now the things of the past because you are aware of your identity, you are the child of the Most High, walking in power, and you are walking in victory.

14. 'Now thanks be unto God who causes us to triumph in Christ and maketh manifest the savour of His knowledge by us in every place.'

– 2 Corinthians 2:14 (KJV).

God is not a man who can lie; whatever He says in His word, He shall perform it without fail. The above verse tells us that He causes us to triumph in Christ in every place, which means whatever you may be going through, do not allow those challenges to disappoint or discourage you. Victory is yours at the end of it all as God has also promised that we are more than conquerors above whatever we may go through. I encourage you today to come out of the life of disappointments and understand that everything is in control; God is still sitting on the throne. God has also promised us that He will never leave us nor forsake us but in every situation, He is going to make a way out and make everything work together for good. The situation you are going through may be very challenging but always avoid staying in disappointment, because disappointments may lead you to discouragement. When you stay too long in discouragement, it can develop into depression; this depression is a sickness that will prevent you from living the life that God has intended for you. If you want to live a triumphal or victorious life, you need to learn to trust in God no matter how challenging your situation can be. When you live a life of discouragement, it may make you start doubting God or lose faith, as you know that, without faith, we cannot please God. This is the weapon that the devil is using against many people, to rob them of experiencing the glorious life that God has planned and prepared for them. I encourage you today not to be a victim of the schemes of the devil, but instead, try to walk in the light of who you are and whose you are. The devil is working diligently to devise some strategies that will make you feel defeated, powerless and overpowered by your circumstances.

The devil is a liar and the father of all lies. His intention is to kill, steal and destroy, but God, through Jesus Christ, causes us to be victorious and to live life to the fullest. The choice is yours; today you can either choose to believe the lie of the devil or choose to believe the truth of God's word about you and live a victorious life. We are all at war, where the enemy is the devil and the battlefield is the mind. The devil knows that once he conquers your mind then he has won the battle and you will never experience the life that God has intended for you. Maybe you might say, 'if you only knew what I have gone through or what I am going through, you would understand how challenging things are'. I may not know what you are going through right now or what you have gone through before, but one thing I know is that, if you put your trust in the Lord, you will come out victorious.

I have never seen anyone putting his or her trust in God and coming out defeated. The Bible says God always causes us to be triumphant through Christ Jesus. The Bible says God always, not sometimes, causes us to be victorious, and He says that He makes all things work together for good. The enemy may attack your thoughts to make you feel like you are already defeated, but always understand that the word defeat does not exist in anyone who knows their identity in Christ. The good and the bad things all work together for good if you can keep the faith. Trust God's plan for your life and understand that you have the DNA of Christ that knows no failure, no defeat, but knows only victory. Maybe, as you are reading this chapter, you feel like the devil has defeated you already, but I want to assure you that God's plans and ways are higher than your ways. What may look like a defeat in your life may be the very thing that God is using to promote you to the next level.

Whatever the devil has meant for evil in your life, God is capable of turning it to your advantage, like the life of Joseph. What his brothers meant for evil for him, God turned it to be the means of positioning Joseph to fulfil his destiny. Understanding your identity of who you are in Christ, makes you realise that you cannot be disadvantaged at any time in your life. The very winds that the enemy had meant to blow you away will be the very winds that will blow you to your destiny and to the levels where God wants you to be. There is a principle that an eagle uses when there is a storm; the eagle will stretch its wings and allow the very winds that are causing the storm on the ground to lift it above the storm. When all other birds are running to hide in nests and branches, the eagle will be resting on the other side of the storm, then, when the storm is over, the eagle will come down. My point is, whatever seems to be a storm in your life can be the very things that God can use to lift you to the next level in your life. Do not let the disappointments and the regrets of yesterday destroy the hopes and the dreams of your tomorrow. May the Apostle Paul's words encourage you when he said 'one thing I do is forget things that are behind me and strain towards the goal that lies ahead of me'. Paul did not have a good history, as he was murderer, persecuted the church of God and put it into waste, but he never allowed his past to destroy what God had planned for him.

David is another biblical example; he committed adultery and he was also a killer, but he did not allow his past mistakes to destroy his future. King David is the one who went on to say, 'surely goodness and mercy shall follow me all the days of my life'. He understood the principle of letting go of the past and focusing on what is ahead. No wonder God said of David that he was a man after His own heart, because David did not dwell in his past mistakes, but he decided to repent and worship God with a pure heart. This is what is required of us to let go of the emotional wounds, bitterness and unforgiveness and run this race called life by focusing ahead and living the life according to how God intended us to live it.

I encourage you to have an attitude like King David and Apostle Paul who, against all odds, decided to let go of the past and focus on what was ahead of them. When you study the life of Apostle Paul and King David, there are some similarities in their lives. Their biggest similarity was greatness. Paul became one the greatest Apostles in the New Testament, wrote most of the books in the New Testament, and established many more churches than any other Apostles. David, on the other hand, became the greatest King in the history of the Bible by being a man that was after God's own heart.

These two great men did what I am encouraging you to do today; they let go of their past negative lives and chose to live the kind of life that God had intended for them. This is the time to put your past behind you. Understand that God starts from barrenness to promise; He also starts from chaos to cosmos, so above everything, always know that you are a daughter and a son of destiny. God is about to do something great in your life.

10b. 'the joy of the Lord is your strength.'

– Nehemiah 8:10b (Amplified version).

The joy of the Lord will enable you to live the life that God has intended for you, and that is the main reason why the devil is bringing or has brought so many things in your life because he wants to steal your joy and make you lose faith. The enemy knows that when you lose your joy, then you will live a frustrated life, and that will lead you to live a life of defeat. The Bible says we are not ignorant of the schemes of the devil because we know who we are in Christ; therefore, this is the time to arise above all odds and walk in the light of who we are in Christ. Worshipping God in the midst of your challenges will give you peace and joy because the Bible tells us that God dwells in the praise of His people. When God is at the scene, no power or force can do you anything; everything else has to pave the way because of the presence of God.

23. 'And when they have laid many stripes upon them, they cast them into the prison, charging the jailer to keep them safely.

24. Who have received such charge, thrust them into the inner prison and made their feet fast in stocks.

25. And at midnight Paul and Silas prayed and sang praises unto God and the prisoners heard them.

26. Suddenly there was a great earthquake, so that the foundations of the prison were shaken and immediately all the doors were opened and everyone's bands were loosed.'

– Acts 16:23-26 (KJV).

Paul and Silas knew that the secret of uplifting the hearts above their troubles was to enter into the presence of God and His power through prayer and singing hymns. When I did some in-depth research about the situation of Paul and Silas, this is what I found out:

1. They were severely beaten

2. The environment was depressing according to the standards of prison during that time.

3. The prison was a dark, damp and stench-ridden place (very smelly) with no facilities for waste or any comfort of any kind.

4. They were locked in the inner prison.

5. They were chained both the hands and feet.

Paul and Silas were experiencing throbbing pain in their bodies and a disheartening atmosphere, but at midnight, they prayed and sang praises to God and their situation changed suddenly. The situation that Paul and Silas went through was a traumatic experience, yet they never allowed that situation to make them bitter; but instead, they both had a clear understanding that it is only keeping the joy and trusting God that would change their situation. They had an understanding that keeping the joy and praising God in the midst of chaos would give them the victory they needed. The main lesson that we learn from the account of Paul and Silas is that regardless of what you have gone through or you are going through, you need to keep the joy and peace and surrender everything to God. Let there be peace in the midst of your storms because God is with you and for you, therefore, nothing can by any means defeat you. The main challenge that many Christians are struggling with is that they allow the storms to affect them on the inside. Today, you may be going through a storm but never allow that storm to get into you and steal your joy and peace and make you lose your focus. You may be going through the storm but always know that you have the DNA of Christ that knows no defeat. When you understand your identity in Christ, even if you are going through storms, you will remain unshakable, unmovable and living the life that God intended for you.

Declarations

- I declare and decree that all things are working together for good; therefore, I am not going to be bound by the spirit of unforgiveness.

- I declare and decree that what the enemy had meant for evil for me, God is turning around for my blessing.

- I declare and decree that what looked like a setback in my life is converted to be a set-up for my great comeback.

- I declare and decree that what looked like a stumbling block is now converted into a stepping stone to my next level of greater achievement.

- I declare and decree that every spirit of bitterness and unforgiveness is uprooted from its roots in Jesus' mighty matchless name; therefore, I am walking in liberty and freedom from unforgiveness.

- I declare and decree that, from this day, I will experience a new sense of freedom, new happiness and new fulfilment because I have decided to let go of the past.

- I declare and decree that rejection, hatred, bitterness and unforgiveness shall be far from my life from now onwards, in Jesus' mighty name.

- I declare and decree that I am lifted above every shame and reproach in my life and a new dawn has started in my life.

- I declare and decree that I have a clear vision for life, destiny and future because I have decided to let go of the hindsight.

- I declare and decree that the eyes of my understanding are enlightened towards the express will of God for my life, therefore, I refuse to hold onto my past emotional wounds and setbacks.

- I declare and decree that all my trials are a unique stepping stone to my sure promotion and victory in Jesus' mighty name.

- I declare and decree that I shall come out of every trial triumphantly because I have allowed God to fight my battles, therefore, sure victory is guaranteed.

- I declare and decree that I am arising and shining for I have received the truth of God's word that brings liberty.

- I declare and decree that, from now onwards, I am going to begin to enjoy divine acceptance where I suffered rejection and abuse before, in Jesus' mighty name.

- I declare and decree that today, I have broken the spirit of bitterness and unforgiveness, therefore from now onwards I am like a tree planted by the river of water; I yield fruits in season and all that I do will prosper.

- I declare and decree that I have the joy and peace, I am not going to let people and circumstances upset me, and I will arise above every challenge knowing that God is on my side, therefore, I am choosing to live my life happy by letting God fight my battles.

Chapter 11.
Understanding Your True Identity in Christ

Understanding your identity in Christ will make you live a victorious life and a life free from strife, bitterness and unforgiveness. When you have a clear knowledge of what rights you have as a child of God and what God can do for you, you will never struggle with letting go of the past.

> *9. 'But you are a chosen race, a royal priesthood, a dedicated nation; (God's) own purchased, special people, that you may set forth the wonderful deeds and display the virtues of Him Who called you out of darkness into His marvellous light.'*

– 1 Peter 2:9 (Amplified version).

God, through His word, is telling us that we are a chosen race, special people and God's own purchased ones; this is an assurance that we are not ordinary people but we are God's very chosen ones. When we come to an understanding of who we are in Christ, we are not going to walk in the realm of the flesh, which is walking in bitterness and unforgiveness. Walking in the realm of bitterness and unforgiveness is simply walking in darkness, which is not our domain because we are no longer children of darkness, but those of light. People who have discovered who there are in Christ will never struggle with letting go of the past because they know that all things work together for good for those who are called according to God's purpose. Walking in bitterness and unforgiveness is an indication that you have not fully understood who you are in Christ. The word of God clearly tells us that those who cannot love people that they see are still walking in darkness.

6. 'And hath made us kings and priests unto God and His father, to Him be the glory and dominion forever and ever. Amen'

Revelation 1:6 (KJV).

10. 'And has made us into our God kings and priests, and we shall reign on earth.'

– Revelation 5:10 (KJV).

The above scriptures tell us that God has made us kings and priests through the finished work of Christ and we are born to reign in this earth. The word of a king or queen has power; what the queen or the king declares must be obeyed or respected as declared. This is the privilege that God has given us because of what Jesus did for us, and therefore we need to walk and talk like kings and queens because this is how God sees us. When a king or queen speaks, their voices have power. Walking with the authority invested in us, we will never struggle with bitterness and unforgiveness but instead, we walk in the newness of our nature in Christ Jesus. The verse above promises us that we shall reign on this earth, with such understanding that you will never hold onto things like strife, malice and bitterness because you know that such things will not allow you to reign. Reigning and walking in dominion will involve the decision of choosing to walk in your identity in Christ, which is walking in love and forgiveness. Things like bitterness and unforgiveness are hindrances and obstacles to you experiencing the life of dominion and victory.

> *20. 'So we are Christ's ambassadors, God is making His appeal through us. We speak for Christ when we plead, 'Come back to God.'*

– 2 Corinthians 5:20 (NIV).

When you look at the above scripture, it clearly states that we are Christ's ambassadors in this world; in other words, it means we are the representative of Christ in this world. This is the reason why we are called Christians, which is derived from the word Christ and this is why Jesus Himself said He is the vine and we are the branches. Understanding that we are Christ's ambassadors in this world will make you live the life of victory that God has intended for you. Many countries have ambassadors representing other countries within their own. When anything happens to that ambassador, the whole country where that ambassador comes from will react on his or her behalf, to find out what has happened. The same analogy applies to all Christians; for anything that happens to you in this world, the whole of heaven will react on your behalf. When you have this understanding about who you are in Christ, you will know that you are untouchable, unmovable and unshakable because you are backed up by the whole of heaven. You are the ambassador of heaven, therefore, all of heaven is behind you and is for you, and because of this, you cannot be defeated; you will accomplish what God has intended in your life. There is no power, no circumstances or demons that can stop what God has planned for you; you just need to understand whose you are and who you are in Christ.

10. 'For we are God's handiwork, created in Christ Jesus to do good works, which God prepared in advance for us to do.'

– Ephesians 2:10(NIV).

The verse above says we have been created in Christ Jesus to do good works that God has prepared for us, and part of the good works is to walk in love by forgiving those who have offended us. Understanding your identity in Christ will make you realise that there is no room for walking in bitterness and unforgiveness because that is not part of the good things that God has prepared for us. All those who still walk in the spirit of bitterness and unforgiveness by not letting go of the past are people or Christians who have not understood their true identity in Christ. As the light of who you are in Christ is dawning in you, this is the time to let go of all the works of the flesh and walk in the fruit of the Spirit.

Understanding God's Promises for You

> 11. '"For I know the plans I have for you," declares the Lord. "Plans to prosper you and not to harm you, plans to give you hope and future".'

– Jeremiah 29:11(KJV).

The verse above explains God's promise for us. He wants to prosper us, give us hope and a future. When you truly understand that you are destined for greatness and your future is bright, you will never allow people and circumstances to rob you of the great things that are ahead of you. God Himself in His word is telling us that His plan is to make us prosper and have a great future. There is no need to walk in defeat or live a hopeless life as that is contrary to what God is saying about us. I believe that this is time to arise on the inside and say 'no matter what I am facing now or what I have gone through in the past, I refuse to give up. My future is bright, I am destined for greatness. I know who I belong to, and I know beyond any doubt that God will never allow me to be put into shame; His word is finally about my life'.

Declarations

- I am born to prosper.

- I am born to be victorious.

- I am born to shine.

- I am born to be great.

- I am born to be an overcomer in Christ Jesus.

- I am born to walk in dominion.

- I am in the palm of God's hands and, as a result, I am fully protected.

- I am the apple of God's eye; anyone who touches me, God will react.

- I know whose I am, a child of the most High God.

- I know who I am in Christ.

- I am a king/queen in the eyes of God; therefore, I have power and authority.

- I am an ambassador of Christ in this world, therefore all of heaven is backing me up. I cannot be defeated.

- The life of Christ is in me; Jesus is the vine and I am the branch that gets its life from the vine.

- Defeat and failure are the things of the past; I can do all things through Christ who strengthens me.

- Bitterness and unforgiveness are not my path because I have the DNA of my heavenly father, which is love.

- I walk in victory, I walk in power and I walk in the light of my true identity in Christ.

14. 'The Lord will fight for you; you need only to be still.'

– Exodus 14:14 (KJV).

'God promises to fight for us, so there is no need to fight for ourselves and end up living a life of bitterness and unforgiveness, but we need to understand that victory is guaranteed because God is fighting our battles. In the battles that God fights, there is a sure guaranteed victory for us.

2. Consider it pure joy, my brothers and sisters, whenever you face trials of any kinds,

3. Because you know that the testing of your faith produces perseverance.

4. Let perseverance finish its work so that you may be mature and complete, not lacking anything.'

– James 1:2-4(KJV).

57. 'But thanks be to God, He gives us the victory through our Lord Jesus Christ.'

– 1 Corinthians 15:57(KJV).

The word of God encourages us to understand that anything that we can face in life works together for our good; some of them are there to give us the experience and to make us mature in Christianity. They say experience is the best teacher, and the things that we experience in life will give us a good standing when it comes to helping others who are going through the same things that we have encountered in life. The good thing is that no matter how hard things we may encounter in life can be, God has already given us victory through Jesus Christ. God has set everything in place in order for us to live the life that He has intended for us, therefore, there is no need to keep on walking in bitterness and unforgiveness, for all things work together for good.

29. *'He gives strength to the weary and increases the power of the weak,*

31. *But those who hope in the Lord will renew their strength. They will soar on wings like eagles, they will run and not grow weary, they will walk and not be faint.'*

– Isaiah 40:29-31(NAS).

10. *'So do not fear, for I am with you; do not be dismayed, for I am your God. I will strengthen you and help you. I will uphold you with my righteous right hand.*

13. *For I am the Lord your God who takes hold of your right hand and says to you, do not fear, I will help you.'*

– Isaiah 41:10,13(NAS).

*17. 'No weapon forged against you will
prevail, and you will refute every tongue that
accuses you. This is the heritage of the
servants of the Lord and this is their
vindication from me, declares the Lord.'*

– Isaiah 54:17(NAS).

God is not like a man; He cannot lie. What He
has said and promised that He will do, He will do. All
the above scriptures tell us about the promises of
God in our lives. If God is for us, who can be against
us? Even when we feel weary, He will give us
strength to live a life that He had intended for us
without fail. Whenever you feel overwhelmed by
situations, always encourage yourself on the
promises of God that assure you not to fear
because He is going to help you and renew your
strength. Whatever you might be going through,
God is with you and for you, and He will be your
vindicator in every situation you are going through.
You must not allow any situation to discourage you
from living the life that God has intended for you
because God encourages us in His word that, above
every situation, we will emerge as overcomers.
Victory is yours today, so square your shoulders, lift
your head high and walk like a king or queen
because this the way that God has programmed you
to be, in life. There is no weapon formed against you
that will prosper; every intention of the devil against

your life is defeated and every negative voice of the enemy is cancelled; that is God's promise for you.

> *13. 'And I will do whatever you ask in my name, so that the Father may be glorified in the Son.*

> *14. You may ask me for anything in my name, and I will do it.*

> *15. If you love me, keep my commands.*

> *16. And I will ask the Father, and he will give you another advocate to help you and be with you forever.'*

> **– John 14:13-16 (KJV).**

The storms that come your way will not destroy you because God is with you and He has given you the Holy Spirit to be your helper. When you are going through challenges, ask God to give you strength to overcome your challenges, as He has promised us that whatever we ask, He will do it. Everything that we need to live the life that God has intended for us is at our disposal, therefore, there is no reason to feel defeated and end up walking in bitterness and unforgiveness.

Chapter 12.

The Power of Your Words

The book of Proverbs 18:21 tells us that the tongue has the power of life or death. Your words can either speak life or death. Our tongues can build up or tear down. The choice is yours; if you choose to speak life then you will have life. Words are also like seeds; when you speak them, they are planted, they germinate, take root and grow to produce the fruits of the same kind. If your words are positive and life-giving words, then you will reap positive results in your life. Words are also self-fulfilling prophecies; whatever you continuously speak, it will eventually manifest in the physical. You can shape the course of your life through words; remember things that do exist came into existence by the power of a spoken word from God. God has given us the same power through our words to be creative.

As I conclude writing this book, I have put together a list of declarations. I hope as you make these declarations by faith, understanding the power of your words, understanding who you are and whose you are, you will experience a great change in your life. I hope to see you at the top.

The Effective Declarations

- I declare and decree that all things are working together for good, therefore I am not going to be bound by the spirit of unforgiveness.

- I declare and decree that what the enemy had meant for evil for me, God is turning it around for my blessing.

- I declare and decree that what looked like a setback in my life is converted to be a set-up for my great comeback.

- I declare and decree that what looked like an obstacle in my life is now converted to be a stepping stone to my next level of greater achievements.

- I declare and decree that every spirit of bitterness and unforgiveness is torn up by its roots in Jesus' mighty matchless name; therefore, I am walking in liberty and freedom from unforgiveness.

- I declare and decree that from this day forward I will experience a new sense of freedom, new happiness and new fulfilment because I have decided to let go of the past.

- I declare and decree that rejection, hatred, bitterness and unforgiveness shall be far from my life from now onwards in Jesus' mighty name.

- I declare and decree that I am lifted above every shame and reproach in my life and a new dawn has started in my life.

- I declare and decree that I have a clear vision for life, destiny and future because I have decided to let go of the hindsight.

- I declare and decree that the eyes of my understanding are enlightened towards the express will of God for my life, therefore I refuse to hold onto my past emotional wounds and setbacks.

- I declare and I decree that all my trials are unique stepping stones to my sure promotion and victory in Jesus' mighty name.

- I declare and decree that I shall come out of every trial triumphantly because I have allowed God to fight my battles, therefore, sure victory is guaranteed.

- I declare and decree that I am arising and shining for I have received the truth of God's word that brings liberty.

- I declare and decree that from now onwards I am going to begin to enjoy divine acceptance where I suffered rejection and abuse before in Jesus' mighty name.

- I declare and decree that today, I have broken the spirit of bitterness and unforgiveness, therefore, from now onwards, I am like a tree planted by the rivers of water; I yield fruits in season and all that I do will prosper.

- I declare and decree that I have the joy and peace. I am not going to let people and circumstances upset me; I will rise above every challenge knowing that God is on my side, therefore, I am choosing to live my life happy and letting God fight my battles.

- I declare and decree that I am born to prosper.

- I declare and decree that I am born to be victorious.

- I declare and decree that I am born to shine.

- I declare and decree that I am born to be great.

- I declare and decree that I am born to be an overcomer in Christ Jesus.

- I declare and decree that I am born to walk in dominion.

- I declare and decree that I am in the palm of God's hands, and, as a result, I am fully protected.

- I declare and decree that I am the apple of God's eye; anyone who touches me, God will react.

- I declare and decree that I know whose I am; I am a child of the Most High God.

- I declare and decree that I know who I am in Christ.

- I declare and decree that I am a king/queen in the eyes of God, therefore, I have power and authority.

- I declare and decree that I am an ambassador of Christ in this world, therefore, all of heaven is backing me up; I cannot be defeated.

- I declare and decree that the life of Christ is in me; Jesus is the Vine and I am the branch that gets life from the vine.

- I declare and decree that defeat and failure are the things of the past; I can do all things through Christ who strengthens me.

- I declare and decree that bitterness and unforgiveness is not my path because I have the DNA of my heavenly father, which is love.

- I declare and decree that I walk in victory, I walk in power and I walk in the light of my identity in Christ.

  See you at the top

Other Books by Phil Sibanda

The True Essence of Christianity

This book contains the basic truths you need to know to be an effective Christian. This book is for both beginners and mature Christians to advance their knowledge in understanding their Christian walk with God.

.

Notes

About the author

Phil Sibanda is an anointed and ordained Pastor; he is the founder of Word Worldwide church with branches in the United Kingdom and America (USA).

Pastor Phil Sibanda is called by God to preach, teach the undiluted word of God, heal the sick and bring liberty to those who are bound by the devil. He has more than a decade in the ministry, establishing churches, teaching, counselling, touching and changing people's lives and destiny. He is a Pastor, visionary, author, motivational speaker, a father, a leader and a TV personality.

He is obedient to his call and ministers wherever God sends him. He is an international preacher in many different countries: Europe, Africa, Asia and America. He is working, on his way to reach every continent, at spreading the good news of Jesus Christ. He has studied Theology at Diploma and Degree levels and he is also a graduate in Psychology and Counselling. He is currently based in England.

Pastor Phil Sibanda cherishes his call in bringing forth the uncompromising Word of God with the gifts upon his life and he has blessed many with the profound truth of the word of God. He is open for invitations in any part of the world for conferences, revivals, crusades and church planting.

Church website:

www.wordworldwideonline.com

Email: spastorphil@yahoo.com

FB: Word worldwide church